Old Dogs, Old Friends

Enjoying Your Older Dog

Old Dogs, Old Friends

Enjoying Your Older Dog

BONNIE WILCOX, DVM
and
CHRIS WALKOWICZ

HOWELL BOOK HOUSE
New York

Maxwell Macmillan Canada
Toronto

Maxwell Macmillan International
New York   Oxford   Singapore   Sydney

Howell Book House
Macmillan Publishing Company
866 Third Avenue
New York, NY 10022

Maxwell Macmillan Canada, Inc.
1200 Eglinton Avenue East
Suite 200
Don Mills, Ontario M3C 3N1

Library of Congress Cataloging-in-Publication Data
Wilcox, Bonnie.
   Old dogs, old friends : enjoying your older dog / Bonnie Wilcox
and Chris Walkowicz.
     p. cm.
   ISBN 0-87605-750-4
   1. Dogs. 2. Dogs—Health. 3. Dogs—Diseases. 4. Veterinary
geriatrics. I. Walkowicz, Chris. II. Title.
SF427.W54   1991
636.7—dc20   91-15788   CIP

Macmillan books are available at special discounts for bulk purchases for sales promotions, premiums, fund-raising, or educational use. For details, contact:

Special Sales Director
Macmillan Publishing Company
866 Third Avenue
New York, NY 10022

10 9 8 7 6 5 4 3 2 1

Printed in the United States of America

*Blessed is the person
who has earned the love
of an old dog.*
SIDNEY JEANNE SEWARD

*Dedicated to old dogs
and the people who love them.*

Chris Walkowicz and Bonnie Wilcox, DVM. Top: CH Arcadia's Marcy of Rich-Lin CD, ROM, Bearded Collie, age 13; CH Edenborough Quick Silver, ROM, ROMI, "Sally," Bearded Collie, age 13; Bottom: Walkoway's Hepburn, "Katie," German Shepherd Dog, age 10; Duke's Hammel V. Muehlenbach UD, "Henry," German Shorthaired Pointer, age 13.

Contents

Foreword

The new puppy, everyone's friend, a single wiggle from head to toe, is all promise. Then, where did the time go, he's all grown up. No longer clumsy, he gaits with purpose now. And better still, he sits, he stays, and the kitchen floor is clean. Mere moments later, or so it seems, his walk is slow and stiff. Where little black whiskers went every which way, now grey ones grow. And so it goes when you let a dog capture your heart. One day you wonder if the ticking clock wrapped in a towel will really work so that you can finally get some sleep, because it's the last thing you know to try on a puppy's first night. And a couple of moments later you notice that the eyes that look so lovingly into yours have become milky and have to strain to see the face, your face, the dearest thing they have ever seen. In the scheme of things, a dog's life seems but a minute long.

The dog who has grown up and old at your side, the promise fulfilled, the dog who has moved, in a single, graceful stroke from being an adorable pain in the neck to becoming a dignified companion, this dog merits our attention to the last.

Knowing this, Bonnie Wilcox and Chris Walkowicz have given us just what we need—an easy-to-read, generous, delightful book full of information about the way to care for older dogs. This wonderful book is full of tips, reminders, cautions, advice, and even inspiration to help us keep our dear old canine friends as happy and healthy as possible for as long as possible. As if that weren't more than enough, the authors have sprinkled in many pertinent personal stories, some funny, some sad, all perfect.

Bravo, authors, from this dog lover and her sweet old girl, Scarlet.

Carol Lea Benjamin
author of MOTHER KNOWS BEST, THE
NATURAL WAY TO TRAIN YOUR DOG

Introduction

A scant few years ago, when you crawled out of a cozy bed for 2:00 A.M. backyard jaunts in answer to demanding puppy squawks, you thought this was a long way off. But one day, seemingly just a moment or two after wiping up the last puppy puddle, you notice a gray whisker on your best friend's muzzle.

Emotion suddenly clouds your vision—you can't bear to think of losing your buddy. You hug him, realizing you've got a gray hair or two yourself. Then he drops his favorite ball at your feet and barks an invitation to play. Hey, there's plenty of life in the old guy yet!

Pets are living longer today. In the past fifty years, their life span has nearly doubled, a cause for rejoicing. A recent veterinary study showed that now, after puppies are weaned (infancy, as in humans, is the greatest danger period), the average life span has increased from 5.1 years to 8.7 years. By the time the dog celebrates his first birthday, life expectancy reaches twelve years of age. In a 1988 survey conducted by *Dog Fancy* magazine, 48 percent of the respondents owned dogs aged ten to twelve. Another 35 percent had thirteen- to fifteen-year-old dogs, and several happily reported having dogs of fifteen to twenty-plus years!

The 1990 edition of the *Guinness Book of World Records* lists an Australian Cattle Dog named Bluey as holding the record for canine longevity, at twenty-nine years, five months. Bluey worked as a stock dog for his owner, Les Hall, in Australia for nearly twenty years! Close on Bluey's heels is Adjutant, a black Labrador Retriever who accompanied his gameskeeper owner, James Hawkes, around the Revesby Estate in England for twenty-seven years, three months.

Even if our pets could triple their life spans, it would still be too soon to lose them. There's never a good time to lose a friend or member of the family. Although it's not so, sometimes it seems as though our dogs age overnight. Susan LaCroix Hamil explains this in an article, "As Time Goes By," in *Dog Fancy* magazine (March 1989). In contrast to human aging, which takes place mainly during the latter one third of our lives and is spread over a period of twenty-five years, the canine equivalent is only four years. Therefore, Hamil says, "Significant changes can occur in your dog's physical appearance and organ systems in as little as three to six months."

As a practicing veterinarian and a dog breeder for more than twenty years, we would like to help others relish and remember the good times with these special dogs and ease the difficulties.

Each of these chapters covers a topic of concern in your relationship with an aging pet: building memories, acquiring an older dog, the active older dog, keeping things the same, adapting to change, health and paying tribute to our old friends. The two health chapters should serve as reference guides for the future.

Aging is not a disease. Some of the best years remain. Why not enjoy this special time with our best friends?

Nugget, a Golden Retriever, has had good care and love all of his fourteen years. Despite his hip dysplasia, he still enjoys playing ball and long walks. Nugget is typical of his breed and loves people and other animals. Jackie says he's so gentle she always thought he'd make a great mother. She adds, "He's nothing special except to me."

And this is why this book was written for those special dogs and the special people who love them.

Old Dogs, Old Friends

Enjoying Your Older Dog

CH/OTCH Merriley's Steely Dan, "Danny," Shetland Sheepdog, age nearly 16 (13 in this picture), 100 BOB by the age of 7, shown in obedience at 12 to obtain his OTCH, at age 12-14 returned to the breed ring to win another 36 BOBs. Won Veterans at National Specialty at age 14½. Owner: Karen & Gene Dickinson, Woodland Hills, CA.

1

Memories Are Forever

The pleasure is not in what's at the end of the road, but in walking down that road.

ARTHUR SCHOPENHAUER

OLD DOGS, like old shoes, are comfortable. They might be a bit out of shape and a little worn around the edges, but they fit well.

Old friends know and accept our idiosyncrasies and our imperfections. And old dogs are the best of friends. They not only accept us as we are, they don't offer advice or criticism. The elderly pet makes few demands upon us and is usually happy to simply curl up by our feet. Pets don't carry tales to others when we fail at a task or behave in a less-than-sterling manner. No wonder some people say, ''The more I know about people, the more I like my dog.''

As you stroke your old guy's head and think about the secrets you have shared over the years, the flood of memories is as soothing as a cool creek on a hot summer day. Memories such as the puppy ecstasy whenever you returned home and the steamy day you shared an ice cream cone. Or the day he ran his first sled race, squinting into the wind, snow and ice coating his face, his inheritance exuberantly urging him on despite bitter cold and inexperience.

A teenager might remember feeding Sheba those detested carrots

This 10-year old dog had just had surgery for mouth cancer shortly before this photo was taken. A year later, she's still enjoying life in good health. Owner: Lynn Boone.

A Nugget of Pyrite, age 14, always picks up something on his walks, doing his part in keeping America beautiful. Owner: Jackie Wyandt.

At age 11, Maggie UD invites you to play a game of Frisbee. Owner: Betty Swenson, DVM.

under the table so Mom would consent to dessert—and that even Sheba wouldn't eat the broccoli!

Or the walk around the block when Alf tried to make friends with a kitten; his puzzled look when his overtures brought only a hiss and a swat on the nose.

When the mother duck introduced her nine little ones to Spicey, recalls Tommie, "she watched us as intently as we watched her. Spicey, you were so still, I thought you were holding your breath."

You might chuckle as you recall the first time you took Hans hunting and he pointed a field mouse. But you can't hold back the proud smile as you think of how he won a major shooting dog stake just a few years later.

How about Shauna's eager return when you called? Spectators unofficially estimated her speed at 90 m.p.h. You wondered if you'd fall over when she jumped up . . . and a couple of times you did.

We, the owners of aging pets, are actually the lucky ones. We've had time to build memories, and—until the last moment—there's always time to create more.

Take Hans hunting again. So what if you must walk slowly and don't find a darned thing except a little field mouse? Let him sniff the ground and enjoy the sun on his back, with the breeze wafting tantalizing smells.

Maybe Shauna's recalls are a little slower now, but enter her in a Veterans Obedience class and blow everyone's minds with her mere 60 m.p.h. recall. So she forgets which side to heel on—who cares? Do it to be together and to plant more memories to bud and bloom forever.

How old is old? Due to the differences in various breeds, old age cannot be generalized. Small dogs tend to live longer than their giant counterparts whose life expectancy is about nine years. Toys often live to be fifteen years old, and medium-sized dogs are in the middle of the age range (about twelve years). The American Kennel Club classifies dogs seven and older as senior citizens in the breed ring, where they may be entered in the Veterans class. Competition in Veterans Obedience classes begins at eight years of age.

As we all know, there is no fountain of youth. From the moment of birth, aging begins. No one travels in the other direction, but as the well-worn saw has it, "It's better than the alternative."

Our canine friends have advantages over us in this aging process. They don't remember what youth was like nor lament wasted time or long-gone svelte figures and physical abilities. They don't fear growing older or dying. No sighing over wrinkles or gray hair. Animals have no concept of yesterday or tomorrow; they live only for today. Thus they're perfectly content being a bit slower, a bit grayer, a bit less active.

Dogs don't grieve when their children grow up or leave home and couldn't care less why they don't come to visit. They don't mope if no one sends a card or brings a present. There's no urge to see the world or to dangle a granddog on their knees. And there's no depression when they see the number of candles on the cake or if they fail to reach a goal set when they were younger. Dogs have no mid-life crises or disappointment when sexual activity decreases or when reproductive organs are surgically removed. Their owners find them increasingly easy to live with as they age.

Mature, healthy dogs are extremely tolerant with the young, whether canine or human. They allow youngsters many liberties. Dogs sometimes grit their teeth or sigh, but when the youthful attention becomes too much, they simply rise and move to another spot.

In the world of dogs, growing older is peaceful. It means gaining privileges pups don't have or more time to sleep in the sun. Maturity often brings free access to the entire house rather than confinement to one or two rooms.

When Satin was young, she lived the life of a show dog: training classes, shampoos and blow drys, long hours in crates traveling, laborious labors and demanding whelps. Now the Afghan sleeps beside her beloved owners' bed on a soft carpet. She takes naps on the couch; no other dog is allowed on the furniture. When "Mom" first noticed the old gal creeping up to rest her bones, "Dad" said, "Aw, let her be, she deserves it."

Now Satin rides in the car whenever she wants, but only when she wants to. If she'd rather stay home to snooze on the couch, she is free to do so. This grandma can visit the kennel's puppies, play a bit, then leave any time she wishes. Once a year she is gussied up, taken to a local show and fussed over by everyone.

Someone said to her owner, "Do you think Satin misses her old glamorous life?" and was answered, "Are you kidding?"

Whether or not they have memories is unknown to us; perhaps they have vague recollections known only to them.

Brandy wasn't as active as she used to be, though content with her pattern: go out, eat, sleep and exchange a few kisses for a tummy rub. But when she slept, she dreamed, and whimpers of anticipation escaped the German Shepherd's graying muzzle.

Dual CH/AFCH Golden West Chucko, GSPCA All-Age Dog of Year at age 9, finished his AFCH at age 11. Owners: Kay and Marlin Thrasher.

CH Ziyadah's Tom Tarleton, a rare Sussex Spaniel, finally found enough competition to attain his Championship at age 9+. Owner: John Robert Lewis, Jr.

Her owner, Ed, says he knows she's dreaming of bygone years and lives past. Those sounds come as she guards long-grown broods against the terrors of the unknown. She relives the time when she was nursemaid for litters of various breeds, as well as half a dozen children and their friends. It was up to her to guide their steps to safety, and she took her job seriously, meeting the school bus each day. Her loving nuzzle taught her charges to share and to play peacefully. The puppies were all taught to fend for themselves if need be, hunting for their dinner—maybe a ten-pound bag of kibble or a meatball under the baby's chair.

As Brandy dreamed of her own past adventures and those of her kind, she might save a family from a burning house or rescue a drowning child or bring a soldier safely home. Or dig through eighteen feet of snow to rescue a party of skiers trapped by an avalanche. Her talented sniffer could find bombs and drug caches, a warring enemy or a lost hiker. From time immemorial, dogs like her have been around and, God willing, Ed says, will be here forever.

WHY ARE DOGS LIVING LONGER?

Animal lovers of today take better care of their pets from the moment they are born. Through increased knowledge, improved pet-care products and advanced medical technology, we are able to enjoy our pets longer than ever before.

More dogs now live in their owners' homes, and those who don't usually have warm, cozy houses of their own. Laws regulating pet control have forced owners to become aware of the fact that Marshall doesn't need "room to run" as much as he needs safe, controlled exercise. Walking dogs on leash or confining them to kennel runs or in fenced yards protects the animals from loss and injury.

The time has finally arrived when dogs are desired for themselves rather than only for the services they can perform. People have realized the therapeutic value of a pet. Purchase of a dog is undertaken with more care and forethought than in former times. We want this animal to be around for a long time. Prospective buyers do research: they read books, visit dog shows, observe others' pets and talk to breeders in order to make a good choice. Many realize it is wise to ask breeders about the longevity of the breed as well as the kennel's individual lines.

In this changing, mobile world, moves are frequent. Family and friends may live far away. It becomes increasingly hard to find anyone who's known you longer than your Bull Terrier Butch has. A job transfer brought you to this city just two years ago, but you've had Butch for thirteen years.

Anthony says Ollie was a present for his youngest son's tenth birthday, but everyone knew how much Anthony had wanted that pup. During the next twelve years, all three kids grew up, went away to school, moved into homes with lives of their own. The dog was Anthony's main source of comfort during his wife's illness and, when she passed away, he said, "Ollie knows me better than anyone else, maybe even better than I know myself."

The relationship with a pet as a cherished family member means that the animal is more than "a dawg for the kids." With that realization, many owners are willing to spend more time and money initially to obtain a well-bred animal with a healthy background. But even today's mixed breed or shelter-rescued animal has advantages over his predecessors.

More often than before, dog food manufacturers sell nutritionally complete products. Containing the proper proteins and vitamins, these foods surpass the table scraps of a bygone era. In addition, many companies offer specialized food for the older dog. These senior citizen diets are based on current nutritional research and are tailored for health and longevity. Today's canine senior has a definite advantage over yesterday's dogs who finished off a dinner of potato peels and gristle by haunting the trash for a bone or two.

Not all domesticated animals are fortunate enough to reach their golden years, however. With eighteen million animals each year facing death on the streets and euthanization in the pounds, many dog owners have seen the light. *Too many unwanted dogs are dying for us to indiscriminately breed more.* The simplest answer to animal overpopulation is to neuter pets.

With this civic-minded decision comes a bonus: spaying or neutering eliminates reproductive diseases and greatly lowers the incidence of genital tumors. Breast tumors occur nearly two hundred times less often in females spayed prior to puberty. Better early than late, but it's never *too* late. At least one case of neutering at the age of seventeen is recorded.

Medical advances have yielded new vaccines to prevent diseases such as rabies and distemper, common in the early part of the twentieth

CH Beautie's Blonde Bomber, at age 8 with her friend, Erin. Owners: Darlene and Walter Stuedemann.

century. Distemper was the number one killer of dogs before 1929, when the vaccine to rid the world of that dread disease was first used. Inoculations are available to make pets resistant to illness and possible fatalities caused by other germs, including parvovirus, coronavirus, hepatitis, Leptospirosis, Bordatella and parainfluenza virus.

Once upon a time, veterinarians saw their canine clients only during emergencies. Now, however, owners frequently bring their dogs in for a checkup and booster shots once or twice a year. With this kind of schedule, problems can be diagnosed earlier during a routine examination, rather than finding them when they are already advanced. Veterinarians can now specialize in surgery, oncology, neurology, dentistry, radiology, cardiology, dermatology, ophthalmology, theriogenology (reproduction) and internal medicine, as well as focusing on various other fields. Chemotherapy, pacemakers, cataract surgery and other technologies have bought us more years with our pets, time that has added quality to our oldster's lives.

Quality time means enjoying those golden years with your pet. Whether you adapt a present activity to your dog's current level of performance and capabilities or begin a newer, slower-paced one, it is important to make the aged pet feel loved and to keep the animal active, enjoying life.

Often the most enthusiastic spectator reaction at a dog show comes during the Veterans classes. These competitions evoke an emotional moment, bringing a tingle to the spine and tears to the eyes. Spectators and owners honor those who have given so much to the breed. These veterans are a doorway to the past and, as the saying goes, you can't know where you're going until you know where you've been. At home or in public puppies may draw attention, but— anyplace, anytime—old dogs invite a caress.

Puppies are fun and adorable no matter what the breed or mix. But they're tiring. They have no sense, for one thing. Pups haven't learned all the rules, and their enthusiasm tends to make them forget the ones they have been taught. And they don't stay puppies for long. Like all God's creatures, they grow up quickly.

But old dogs . . . well, they're more mellow, content with life and quieter about their pleasures. They're quite patient, willing to wait their turn in the pattern of things, and their eyes shine with a love not yet visible in a puppy's.

The youngster is indiscriminate, greeting strangers with almost as much excitement as they welcome you. Old dogs are dignified in greeting others, but when they share a moment of affection with you, they look into your heart and give you theirs.

Beth had found the dog at a roadside mountain spring where she had been abandoned. Beth named her Spring. She says, "Her only job in life was to be my companion and friend, but she did that to perfection for the following thirteen years."

While puppies and young adults bounce over for a pat, then *boinnnnnnng* away after a toy, that old guy is happiest when he's with you. Although they may have a cozy nap area or a favorite toy, you have become his all, the reason for his existence.

Jody doted on her Irish Wolfhound, O'Reilly. He stretched out beside the chair in her office whenever she worked on the computer. The data processing she did at home was paid by the hour and brought in extra income for the family. Jody remembered five years ago when she was constantly interrupted from her work by the puppy's mournful plea to play, or to let him out, or to check and see what he was chewing on this time. Not that she minded much, but it sure was easier now. O'Reilly snoozed until she was ready for a break, when they'd both go stretch their legs. If her pet wandered into another room, she didn't have to follow, because he was dependable and well trained. And that made her paychecks more reliable as well. Besides, O'Reilly was good company.

Your old gal keeps your feet warm by resting her chin on them when you read a book. She cozies up beside you on the once-forbidden sofa and protects you from your favorite horror flicks. You barely notice the dent in the cushions, except that you automatically sit on the left side because the right side is hers.

The gnawed table leg and puddles are a faded memory. It's hard to recall a time when Spike had all his teeth, let alone used them on anything but his food. And you swear he was housebroken in two days, just two days! In fact, Spike is quite perfect . . . and he always has been. Now and then he is forgetful, but the nice thing is, he doesn't notice when you forget something—unless it's a nudge to remind you about dinner or that it's time for another pat.

TUNED IN TO EACH OTHER

Old dogs are tuned in to you, your household, your life-style. *Whenever Terri dug her lipstick out of her purse and put it on,*

Lauryn gives 13-year-old Marcy, a Bearded Collie, a hug after the dog's new "easy-do" haircut. Owner: Terri Barnes.

Senior citizens Shep, 17, and Frank Tomcheson, 77. *Renee Stockdale*

her Bearded Collie, Marcy, nearly danced for joy. Terri always took the old Beardie along when errands needed to be run, and riding in the car was one of Marcy's greatest passions. When they passed their favorite fast-food place, Marcy came to attention. She knew she'd share the last bite of Terri's burger.

But why was lipstick the catalyst? Finally, Terri realized she never bothered with lipstick when she spent the day at home.

Although old dogs are sensitive to you and sensible about your requests, they tend to be creatures of habit and enjoy their comforts. Other dogs seem to recognize their status as matriarch or patriarch.

Every night as her owner went to bed, Scarlet the Irish Setter curled up on "her" rug, and Virginia covered the old dog with "her" blanket. One cold night, Virginia awoke and glanced over at Scarlet. The dog was snoring contentedly, but the blanket had slipped off. Just as Virginia began to climb out of her cozy bed, her other dog, Dazy, walked over and tugged the blanket back into place with her teeth, lying down beside her companion. Scarlet's owner lay back, knowing that Dazy was helping to care for their friend.

It's true that caring for an old dog takes time. It's important to routinely groom them and to conduct a home examination for any changes. Sometimes they need to be walked more frequently, and keeping up with medicine doses may tax your memory.

Joe sees humor in the situation. "His pills and mine are lined up next to the vitamins on the breakfast table. First I give Reno his vitamin, then I take mine. While I eat my breakfast, Reno has his. We take our rainbow of pills, three for me, two for him. I swallow mine with juice; Reno prefers a liverwurst chaser. Then he 'rinses' the dishes and I stack them in the dishwasher. Following this routine, we take our first walk of the day, brisk and filled with purpose. Reno gamely tries to cover all the other dogs' territorial marks, squeezing out a drop or two on each spot.

"When we arrive home, I do my chores and Reno does his. First he brings me the paper to read during lunch. Second, he takes his toys out of the box and lines them up, seriously considering which one will be honored with his attention for the day. After we pick up the lunch crumbs, we take a walk in the other direction, slower this time, stopping to smell the flowers along the way. I chat with my friend Harry next door and pass the time of day with other neighbors. Reno sits patiently waiting for the ear rub he always receives from Harry and pats from all the others.

Captain Cory, the Salty Dog, (far left) shows the ropes to her crew. In her eleven years, she's sailed on five boats and both coasts. Owner: Linda Denlinger.

"A.J.," age 7, a Great Dane/St. Bernard mix, receives a kiss from his best buddy Harvey. Applejack's owners are James and Kathy Cox.

OTCH Topbrass Ric O'Shay Barty WCX had 159 High in Trials during his career, with a perfect 200 score at age 11½. Ric won a runoff for HIT against his son on his twelfth birthday. Owners: Sharon and Tom Long.

"Reno sits beside me in the navigator's seat while we make a brief run into town for necessaries, making sure we remember all the important stops: the grocery store for dog food—and liverwurst; the butcher for the knucklebone of the week; and the pet store for a new collar. He even accepts his twice yearly visit at the vet's with dignity.

"Occasionally we take our afternoon walk in town along the river, and while this is an interesting diversion now and again, we prefer our old haunts. When we arrive home, we sit in the backyard, enjoying the sun and 'resting our eyes' now and then. Refreshed, we fix dinner, each eating less red meat, more bran and green crunchy things. After dishes, I watch a bit of TV (Reno likes old westerns) or play a game of gin rummy with Harry while Reno watches to make sure Harry doesn't cheat. We all take one more stroll around the lawn.

"Before bedtime, Reno gathers his toys and puts them in his box, just like I taught him when he was a pup. Each night, when I have to answer nature's call, I let him out the back door to take care of his increased need also, watching so he doesn't wander—which, of course, he never does. He's back in a flash; Reno knows which side of the fence is greener.

"It seems like a dull life to most people, I guess, but we like it. He's even more a part of my life than Harry."

Some things become more precious as they age. Old wines are more flavorful. Coins, stamps and baseball cards increase in value. Long marriages and business associations are celebrated with delight. Antique furniture is shown off with pride.

As free-lance writer Barbara Bush said, "An old dog who has served you long and well is like an old painting. The patina of age softens and beautifies, and like a master's work, can never be replaced by exactly the same thing, ever again."*

* "Old Friends Are the Best," *Pure-Bred Dogs/American Kennel Gazette*, February 1983.

2

Grow Old with Me

Grow old with me!
The best is yet to be . . .
ROBERT BROWNING

WHEN PEOPLE first consider adding a dog to their family, most tend to think of puppies. As with human adoptions, the expectant family wishes to share everything from the beginning. They want to experience the joy of cuddling a tiny, perfect, adorable infant.

Canine—like human—infants aren't always perfect, however. They drool, they piddle (a lot), they spill their food and then sit in it or smash it into their hair. When teething, they sink their needle-sharp teeth into soft parts of your body. Babies sleep when you want to play with them, and they wake when you want to sleep. Young people and dogs both experience an inexplicable attraction to mud, rain puddles and other messy things. The sloppier the better.

They behave their worst just when you want to show them off. At times they are frightened, and you must comfort them. At other times their escapades frighten you and there is little comfort.

Once a person has endured all of these joys (especially two or three or five times), she may wish to cherish and remember them in her heart rather than underfoot. Not all people want to tread that path again.

Dapper was adopted from a shelter at age 8. This Whippet's ears would disqualify him in the show ring, but their expressiveness are a plus for his therapy work. When his ears go up, everyone laughs. Owner/credit: Jacque Schultz.

Maltese Dazzlyn Sir Frost UDT, Can. CDX, TD, earned his UD at age 11 and his Tracking title a year later showing that old dogs can often retain their physical soundness. Owner: Betty Drobac. *Olan Mills*

CHOOSING THE OLDER DOG

Parents sometimes admit they enjoy their children more when the kids are a bit older—as preteens, teenagers or even adults. Veteran dog owners also might prefer the age of reason, the time when the animal becomes that best friend they were looking for. They, unlike new parents, have a choice and can skip right over the frustrations of housebreaking, cutting teeth and middle-of-the-night yowls by adopting an older dog.

Life-styles change. When your schedule demands concentration or long hours, it's not easy to train a pup in the social amenities. An adult dog won't be as likely to cut his teeth on antique chair legs or electrical cords. He's able to last several hours without answering nature's call. He might even protect your property once he decides that's his job.

The same qualities you might seek in a puppy should be apparent in an older dog: a personality that suits you and the capability to be a good companion. Basic mental and physical soundness (allowing for temporary problems perhaps induced by stress) are important. It does no one any good to adopt a dog who is doomed to a life of terror, instability or illness.

If you decide to look for an older dog, he will stick out like a petunia in an onion patch. Search the shelters in your area and ask your veterinarian to keep an eye out. Hard as it is to believe, animals are sometimes abandoned at veterinary clinics or boarding kennels. You'll know when you see the right dog. An invisible bond is there from the start and remains forever.

When Glenda first saw Laddie, he was tied in the backyard of a young, harassed mother. What was Glenda even doing there? She'd always had smooth-coated little dogs, Chihuahuas, and here she was, at a friend's suggestion, looking at the sad eyes of a middle-aged Sheltie who'd been dubbed "King" when he'd been adopted less than a month before.

She wrote, "There at the end of a stretch of knotted string, looking downcast and decidedly miserable, sat a sable Sheltie. Larger than some, but with breeding apparent in the refined head and well-proportioned body, he did indeed present a regal appearance. But there was something else: an aura of weariness, a tangible acknowledgment of having lived an existence that did not exactly coincide with the stately title he had so recently acquired. My friend was right—I could not abandon him. Something between us clicked and our lives were to be united for the next five years."

First she renamed him, then he retrained her: how to bathe a "large" dog, how to groom (turning patiently from side to side), an introduction to obedience classes. Glenda's job required extended travel, and Laddie joined her on the trips. She says he adapted so well that one day she left a meeting, still wrapped up in her thoughts, when she realized somebody was missing. "When I returned to claim him, he nonchalantly appeared, stretching languidly as he emerged from under the conference table . . . confident that I would return."

THE RESCUE DOG

Breed clubs often have rescue operations that save dogs from "over-busy" or abusive homes and from death before their time. These organizations save dogs from pounds, puppy mills and pet shops. They find abandoned animals tied to trees or running down a highway. Members provide foster homes, cleaning and grooming, pay for veterinary care and supply the orphan with much-needed food and affection until an adoptive home can be found. Breed clubs and rescue organizations are listed with the American Kennel Club* and are published in various dog magazines.

The people who have been providing interim care (until *you* came) for the dog might be able to fill in some blanks concerning its history and personality. They can tell you why the dog is looking for a home, whether the shots are current and how the dog reacts to people and other animals.

It isn't always people who make the decision, however, to adopt an older, wiser pet. Sometimes the animal chooses a home by wandering into the yard or showing up at just the right time, almost as if it was psychic and knew you needed a friend.

Rudolph was hanging around Bob's yard when he arrived home from the hospital after visiting his best friend Frank, who was dying. What a Christmas this was. Bob could barely see through his tears as he walked to the front door. He thought he was going crazy because it looked as though there were a reindeer standing beside the house. As he neared the door, Bob saw it was just a dog, a dog with a thorny

---

* American Kennel Club, 51 Madison Avenue, New York, NY 10010, (212) 696-8200.

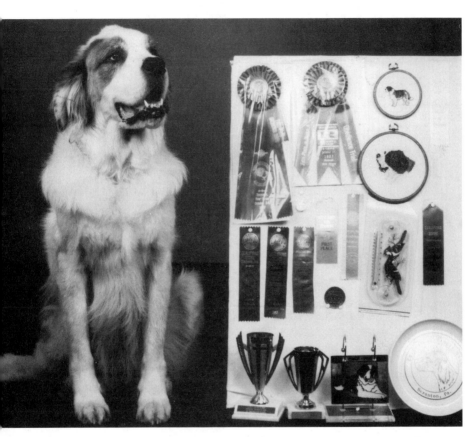

A rescue dog, Dulcinea CD, age 10, shows off her trophies. Owners: Walter and Elizabeth Elvidge.

Due to his owner's illness, Barne
needed to find a new home at age 6
an advanced age for Bulldogs. Owners
Kevin and Louise Wright.

Shih Tzu CH Heavenly Dynasty's T'ai Tzu at age 12. Owner: Jo Ann White.

branch caught in is collar, cuts on his neck . . . and the oddest red nose.

"What could I do?" Bob asks. "It was Christmas Day. There was no one at the pound or at the vet's. I removed the branch, took him in, cleaned up his cuts and shared my Christmas pizza with him. Later that night, when I felt particularly bad, the dog came up and nudged me with that funny nose.

"The first thing that came to my mind was Rudolph and, in my grief over Frank, I began laughing, then crying. Then I felt a rough tongue licking away my tears. I held that dog in my arms all night long."

The following day Bob took the dog to the vet, who pronounced him healthy—thin, but in overall good shape for a stray dog about eight or nine years old. The vet also mentioned, "Funny, you don't see many Vizslas, let alone one running loose."

So Bob knew the dog was a Vizsla, thus the red nose. Rudolph was homeless and old and tired. "But I figured he was sent to me for a reason, so Rudolph and I bypassed the pound and went home together."

When you adopt an adult dog, you can already see what he looks like—no surprise about how big he'll become—and you'll have fewer worries about congenital problems or disease. Most hereditary ailments become apparent by the time the dog is a year or two old.

If he isn't already housebroken, he can be in short order, simply because his bladder can hold more than a tiny pup's. He may already been taught basic obedience, but whether or not he knows "sit," "come" and "down," he'll learn quickly because his attention span is longer than when he was young.

THE OLDER DOG

"Frenchie came to live with the Reilly family on December 27, 1980. She was found on the porch in the early morning by my sister, Mary. Frenchie was very cold and scared; it was unclear how long she was on the porch. She seemed glad to be invited in. After several fruitless attempts to find her owner, she joined the household of an aging Labrador Retriever and three cats."

Margaret's family took the Poodle to their vet, who estimated that she was around five or six years old. Now, ten years later, Mar-

garet says, "Frenchie has added so much to our lives. I'm glad her owners never came for her."

The answers to your questions are all there. Is the dog bold or timid? Calm or excitable? Does the dog bark a lot? Is the coat long or short? You can learn in advance just how often you'll have to groom and whether the coat sheds on navy blue cashmere. In computerese, it's called WYSIWYG: *What you see is what you get.*

Even when you don't know for sure what mix the dog is, an adult's physical characteristics are complete. It's up to you whether or not to play sleuth and track down further information.

One look won't tell you everything, but it can hint. It's like peeking inside the cover of an intriguing book in a store. When you take it home, inside is a whole new world, one that you can enjoy learning about page by page, day by day.

Debra states, "I was not a dog person until Satan, a hundred-pound black and tan Doberman Pinscher that was already ten years old, came to live with us." Debra and her husband proceeded to rename the old dog Harry, to spoil him and to delight in his passions.

She remembers his idiosyncrasies fondly, all now cherished memories. "He did more in his last four years than he did the rest of his life."

Although Dobes are not bred to hunt, Harry loved to hunt 'possums and frogs. He also enjoyed the beach, where he played in the surf, sat in the boat and rode in the Jeep. "I always had to ride in the backseat," Debra says with a laugh, "because he had to ride in the front with my husband. Have you ever tried to move a hundred-pound, spoiled, stubborn Doberman who did not want to move?"

Those were Harry's loves. What he hated were bath days. On Thursdays Debra always came home from work to find Harry "hiding" behind a tree, his head behind the tree, the rest sticking out. He also hated having his bedding washed and would follow her mournfully to the washer in fear his bed would be ruined.

Debra says, "Harry was a wonderful dog with a great sense of humor. I will never forget him. Having him made me a true dog lover. I have two secondhand dogs now."

An ad in the classified section of a newspaper evokes sad images when it reads, "Eight-year-old Collie. Loves kids." For those of us who consider our dog a member of the family, we can't imagine parting with one, especially one who had been with us for eight years. Whatever would make someone give up such an old dog? Grown dogs

Bo was an abused animal prior to her adoption. At age 9, she still loves to hunt and walk in the woods. Owner: Linda Parsons.

Su-Tops Peanut Brittle, Welsh Terrier, at age 16, can still catch anything that is slightly slower than she is. Owner: Eric Ravett.

may be available for adoption for any number of reasons, but it's particularly sad when an old pet is looking for a new home.

An older animal is so often passed over for the young ones. Yet old dogs have so much to offer. They're wise. They're appreciative.

Ben Franklin wrote to a young friend giving advice about the choice of a mistress, ". . . in all your Amours you should prefer old Women to young ones . . . Because they have more Knowledge of the World, and their Minds are better stor'd with Observations. . . . They learn to do a thousand Services small & great, and are the most tender and useful of Friends when you are sick . . . and . . . They are so grateful!''

Whether or not Ben was right about women, old dogs *are* grateful. As they sit in a shelter or pound, they watch those who pass them by giving little heed to what these dogs know and the love they have to share. The eyes of an old dog show a wistfulness. "Stop, wait," they speak silently. And when you do stop, it's hard to say no to a pair of deep, soulful eyes with an almost hopeless look . . . almost, but not quite.

While the pups and youngsters yap and cry for attention, jumping at the kennel door pleading to be chosen, the older dog gives a tentative wag when someone approaches. He does not give his heart as freely as the noisy, fickle young. When he does, it will be totally. He sits patiently waiting for the right person, the one who knows what this wise old dog has to give.

Cathy Jo volunteered at an animal shelter. She was working through her grief at losing her own ten-, thirteen- and sixteen-year-old dogs all within one year. A white Standard Poodle had been found starving, matted, injured and about to be shot. Cathy took Dolly home because she was too large to fit comfortably in the shelter's pen. Her age was estimated at five to seven years.

Three years later Cathy says, "Dolly is grateful. Dolly is gentle and friendly, but she never pushes her way to food or affection or anything else. Dolly is concerned, it is very obvious, with not rocking the boat. We can't explain to her that never, under any circumstances, would she be abandoned again. We bought her a luxury dog bed, which she loves; her meals are on time; she's been given love and care, but she is more of a guest, careful and always, always on her best behavior.''

The experience with Dolly has been so rewarding that next came Lady, a Golden mix, then a few months later, Mimi, a Pekingese. Both

At age 15, grand dam Deja Vu still tries to please owner Jill Hurst.

Cricket, age 11, brightens the day of an Alzheimer's patient who once raised Champion Chihuahuas. Owner: Catherine Weikart.

Blake, rescued after seven years in a shelter. Owner: Judie Chudy.

14-year-old littermates Pixie and Dawn are both Champion Australian Terriers. Owner: Eve Lewis.

were ten years old and had nobody left who cared. Now they do. And Mimi has Cathy wound around her little toe.

Becoming a foster family isn't always simple. It takes time to win trust. It's not easy for the dogs, either. A dog who has led a miserable existence for much of its life is apprehensive that the new luxury bed or rug might be jerked out from under her again. Dogs who have been abandoned or abused may fear "rocking the boat," as Dolly did.

Dumbo seems an unlikely name for a two-pound Maltese, but she was named for the way her ears flapped when she ran. The former owner didn't know for sure how old she was—"eight or nine." Nancy was afraid to take such an old dog, but Dumbo had lost her litter of premature puppies, who had frozen to death outside. "I kept thinking of that poor little dog out in the cold." So Nancy rescued her and gave the dog a name, a home and love.

Nancy and Dumbo spent a lot of time at the vet's, clearing up tapeworms, flea infestation and infections in eyes, ears and teeth. When Dumbo was well enough, her bad teeth were removed and she was spayed. Nancy says, "She's the most affectionate dog I've ever had." No wonder. Nancy was her savior.

The elderly are often set in their ways and used to their routine. When an older dog is adopted, he must adapt to a new schedule and learn different household rules.

But, the owners say, it's all worth it. The dogs don't have to say a thing. They're just grateful.

Blake had just about had it. He'd lived most of his life behind bars at a no-kill animal shelter, and he hated the confinement. His scarred face, torn ear and ground-down nubs of teeth showed proof of his multiple escape attempts. He climbed fences, chewed through wooden walls and scrambled on top of the kennel roof. Life as a stray hadn't been so hot, either. An eye infection had been so bad that, when he was rescued, his eye had to be removed.

So what hope would a ten-year-old, one-eyed, scarred, lop-eared, delinquent hound dog have after seven and a half years of hopelessness? None.

None, that is, until Judie came along. She decided he deserved to live out the rest of his life without looking through a kennel door. Despite his term as a jailbird, Blake had lots of things going for him. He still had a good temperament, was 90 percent housebroken and was friendly with other animals.

So Judie took a chance. She thought Blake deserved that much.

The 10 percent that wasn't housebroken almost did them both in. But, after numerous attempts at confining him to the kitchen, she gave up and decided to let him have the run of the house. It worked. She thinks he probably realized that if he wanted to sleep on the couch he had better be good.

Both Cathy and Judie realize the time left with their animals is shorter than if they'd chosen a younger one, but they think it's worth it. Cathy says, "The joy of having them, even if only for a few years, outweighs the sadness. And I hope, when I finally do lose them, that the joy will ease the pain."

She's not the only one. Cathy notes that during her work at the shelter, she has witnessed many adoptions of adults, some elderly, blind, three-legged or deaf. "Perhaps it's just that only especially kind people will devote the patience necessary to an older animal, or one with problems, but these adoptions always work out beautifully. Inevitably, the people will say, as I do, that they have derived so much more from the relationship than they have given; that the love and gratitude from the animal warms their days and nights; that they don't understand how the former owners could ever have given them up."

But the owners have not always given them up willingly. Career and personal problems, such as moves, divorces or changes in housing regulations, can create situations that force an owner to give up a much-loved pet, causing as much pain to the former owner as to the animal. Sometimes the death or incapacity of the owner leaves the dog without master or home.

CAREER CHANGES FOR DOGS

Although stressful for everyone at the time, there is a silver lining behind this cloud too. It means that not all dogs are available for adoption only because they're delinquents, destructive or defective.

When Rosie hurt her back, she knew she couldn't possibly take care of eleven dogs anymore. Rosie showed and bred her Bedlingtons and loved every one, but some had to go. She had to place some and she did, carefully and selectively, after great consternation.

It was a difficult decision for Rosie, made, as she said, "in physical and mental agony and turmoil."

Who stayed? The three old-timers, definitely, and one youngster to keep them and Rosie young at heart.

Hobby breeders and show kennels may find it necessary, like Rosie, to place their dogs. Occasionally they consider finding retirement homes for dogs that will no longer be shown or bred. Even though it is always a sorrow to part with animals who have played a major role in owners' lives, it is sometimes advisable for their own welfare. Walls only expand so far, and if a new young star hovers over the horizon, sometimes sacrifices have to be made. Even if space and finances are not limited, time is. No matter how wealthy a person is or how spacious his estate, there are still only twenty-four hours in a day. Like it or not, even though an owner of a show kennel gamely makes an effort to divide attention, the retired set is often short-changed.

Although we intend to stop and smell the roses with a golden oldie, it all too rarely happens. He should have a home where he will receive a lion's portion of the attention instead of vying with the young cubs for his share.

Betty adopted Pojo, a champion Cairn Terrier, when he was eight. She thought she'd train him in obedience, but he did all work under protest, so she gave up and instead took him on nursing home visits. When he was thirteen, Betty discovered a recipe for "Beardie Brownies," which Pojo was crazy about. Suddenly, training wasn't so awful!

His owner thought she might receive some criticism for "making such an old dog work," but he danced along beside her, winning enthusiastic support. At six weeks short of fourteen, Pojo became dual titled. Betty says, "Between the petting and cuddling he gets at nursing homes and the attention and activity he gets from his obedience work, it's made a new man of him."

Good homes are also sought by kennel owners who are retiring or moving. And good homes are provided by people who are aware of these situations, such as the editor of one dog magazine who always has a superb terrier living with him. The dogs move with utter contentment from the Best in Show ring to Dan's home and from winning trophies and rosettes to winning Dan's praises.

These ex-show dogs are prime candidates for adoptions because they're usually well trained and have been given the best of care. They've been socialized at training classes and shows and are happy, outgoing animals, used to hustle and bustle.

Since fanciers know in advance they will be seeking a retirement home for a senior, they can be selective in choosing the home. These dogs are rarely advertised. Breeders wait for the ideal person to come

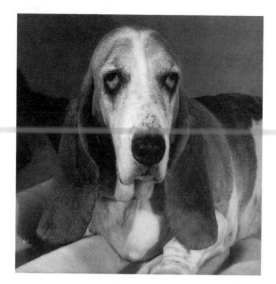

Tiffany flew from New Mexico to Pennsylvania to a new home and owner at age 8. Owner: Sandi Coble. *Linda & Philip Malin*

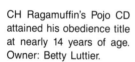

CH Ragamuffin's Pojo CD attained his obedience title at nearly 14 years of age. Owner: Betty Luttier.

to them. Calls and visits from prospective buyers are routine, and the network between kennel club members or fanciers of a particular breed works in the best interest of the dog.

Sandi writes, *"A friend told me that her brother living in Albuquerque, New Mexico, was being promoted and would be traveling a great deal. He had a Basset that he would have to find a home for.*

"I had always loved Bassets," Sandi said, *"so I adopted Tiffany sight unseen when she was eight years old. She arrived in Lancaster, Pennsylvania, a whopping seventy-eight pounds, but with the help of a good 'light' dog food, moderate exercise and a few less treats, she is now a svelte fifty-six pounds and still going strong. Even people who don't like dogs succumb to her charm."*

Sandi added that Tiffany awakened her long dormant interest in the dog world, and she now has a second Basset and is actively showing in Breed, Obedience and Agility competitions.

Occasionally, a visitor strikes up a rapport with one of the older dogs. "It's as though P.B. chose her future home herself," one breeder said.

FOSTER HOMES

Sadly, many people have not made arrangements for placement of their dogs in emergency situations. We dog lovers generally prepare ourselves to lose our pets. Dogs only live a decade or so, and we know that mourning their loss is inevitable. Yet we're all vulnerable too. Death or illness can strike anyone at any time. Since true dog lovers always have a pet, the kindest thing we can do is prepare for that possibility. This is a bewildering and upsetting time for a pet, especially an older one. We can make their adjustment smoother.

Arrange a foster home with someone who not only agrees to be a caretaker but genuinely likes Fluffy—and make sure the feeling is mutual. Store papers and instructions in an accessible place and give a copy to the guardian and to your veterinarian. Note the dog's schedule so that it can be disrupted as little as possible. If Fluffy eats dry food every day, mixed with a bit of meat twice a week and fish on Friday, write that down. Include medication dosage, medical history and the inoculation record.

If we don't make arrangements for the care of our pet, the animal's fate may not be what we would choose. Animal control officers estimate they are called in about 40 percent of the cases involving death of pet owners.

Even worse, the animal may be forgotten in the confusion and turmoil following a death or hospitalization. The dog could spend days suffering—perhaps even die—before someone remembers. What a terrible end for an old friend.

Naming a guardian eliminates any such possibility. A trust fund that provides for food and veterinary care should be arranged to take any financial burden off the caretaker. The trust should be within reason, so that irate relatives don't begrudge Blackie's bequest. A statement of intent outlining your exact wishes should be drawn up and attached to your will, with copies given to a friend, neighbor, relative and veterinarian. Someone should be appointed for immediate as well as long-term care.

"She was originally owned by a neighbor living across the street from where I grew up. As a child, I would borrow her to take on walks and spend long hours with, for I had no dog of my own," Claudia writes.

"Her owner died when she was eight and relatives asked if I would adopt her. They felt that no one would want an older dog and if I would not take her, they would have her put down. She became our loving family pet.

"As a teen, I joined 4-H, training her when she was twelve years old for Showmanship and Obedience competition. We competed until I entered college. She fooled us all and lived into her nineteenth year."

If there is more than one dog, pictures and a physical description should also be placed in the file. When a pet had burdensome physical needs or would not adjust to a new home, you may elect to have your dog euthanized. But that decision should be yours, not someone else's. Even if plans are not made, however, tragedy can still be averted if the relatives or friends know to alert a local dog club, which may be able to arrange a foster home until a permanent owner comes along. We arrange caretakers for our children, yet sometimes forget the needs of the canine member of the family.

We can make this rocky road as smooth as possible for our pet and a guardian by encouraging the animal to interact and perhaps even visit with this person.

Sidney Jeanne loves dogs. She always has and always will. She'll always have one and, at age seventy-five, just bought another. Sidney is active and in good health, but she's realistic. "I know I won't live forever, so my younger friend Katie has promised she'll care for my dogs if anything happens to me. Of course,'' she adds with a twinkle in her eyes, "if I outlive Katie, I'll care for hers too!''

Sidney and Katie visit frequently and, over the years, have "shared'' ownership duties and joys of more than one dog. When one goes out of town, the other dog sits, and a neighbor takes over when they travel together. "Everyone loves everyone,'' says Sidney. "The only problem is this last little demon—I don't know if anyone else can keep up with her!''

That kind of youthful exuberance, enthusiasm and energy is why some people choose an adult dog over a puppy as they themselves age. They relate well to each other, these old folks.

A UNIQUE SOLUTION

Even teaching institutions are discovering the need of pets for care after their owners are gone. The Veterinary School at Texas A&M has recently announced plans for a privately funded Companion Animal Geriatric Center (CAGC), which would provide a homelike setting for older dogs whose owners have died. Veterinary students and the staff will live at the CAGC with the animals. This will provide the care and companionship the dogs need and will also give the students an opportunity to observe and learn about geriatric dogs.

A CHANGE OF COURSE

When Peppy's elderly owners died, Carole rescued the Silky Terrier, who had been left in the couple's backyard with a neighbor feeding him. She was told that he was about seven years old. Several months later, she received the transfer of AKC papers and found that he was actually eleven.

Originally, Peppy just attended Obedience classes with Carole for socialization purposes. But the temptation was too great, and eventually Peppy was bouncing along at the heel position. At thirteen years, Peppy added a C.D. (Companion Dog) title to his name.

Throughout our lives, we often face circumstances that can throw us, and therefore our dogs, into a tizzy: disruption of feeding and exercise routine, extended work hours, a move, a divorce, hospital-

Peppy Jay Mathis CD was rescued at age 11 after his elderly owners died and achieved his Companion Dog title with new owner, Carol Foth.

ization or institutionalization of the owner and, of course, death. Even happy events such as the arrival of a new baby, another pet or a wedding can disrupt everyone just when we've gotten used to a pattern.

When Celia married Ted, she thought they'd be a happy family of three. She'd had her Min Pin, Angel, ever since she was twelve. Angel had been her shadow ever since, slept beside Celia on her bed and curled in her lap as she did homework.

Angel had only one sin. She didn't like men. She tolerated Celia's dad, Charley, but she much preferred Celia's mom and doted on "her girl." (Celia's dad sometimes called the trio "Charley's Angels.") When Celia was at school, Angel waited by the door at precisely 3:30 P.M. For the past six years, the homecoming had been at 5:30 P.M. When Celia dated, Angel ignored the boys. When Ted began spending a great deal of time with Celia, Angel pouted. But Celia thought Angel would learn to tolerate Ted as part of the family too.

Angel didn't and the situation deteriorated, while Ted, in an attempt at humor, started calling the little dog She-Devil. Finally Celia called her mother in tears. Angel had chewed up Ted's favorite slippers, bit Ted's leg when he came home and kissed his new wife, and had even growled at Celia when she shut the dog out of the bedroom.

What could she do? Angel had been her best friend for twelve years, but Ted was her husband.

Poor Celia. Poor Angel. Poor Ted.

Luckily, Celia's mother gladly welcomed the "fallen" Angel home again. Celia took Angel for long walks whenever they visited. She spent quality time with her dog for an hour or so, and Ted was content to leave them alone for the time. Eventually Angel tolerated Ted on the walks too and even deigned to allow him to throw her ball now and then.

Not everyone is as lucky as Celia. Not everyone has a family to take the dog, or a husband as patient as Ted. When situations become intolerable, a solution is needed.

Anticipating these problems may help avoid them. A weaning period to introduce new routines, people and places often helps, particularly with an older dog who has known only one situation for many years. Owners should make changes slowly, first training the dog to sleep on the floor or in a crate, and altering the time they arrive home each night. If possible, an animal should be taken to the new living quarters several times before an actual move. Ted could have spent

Precious, a Beagle age 18, welcomed her owner's new husband. Owner: Melanie Sporer.

Haiku Solar Eclipse UDT spent the first eight years of his life living on a 50-foot sailboat. Now "Teak" has four paws on the ground and is still active in Obedience at age 11. Owner: Martha Fast.

CH Major Acres Branwyn FCH. The only Irish Wolfhound in the history of the breed to win a Specialty BOB at age 9 or older. Maggie's last of four Specialty BOBs was at age 10. Owners Yvonne and Richard Heskett.

time trying to court not only Celia but Angel before the wedding. Tossing the dog's favorite toy, offering a treat and accompanying the two on walks could have helped Angel accept Ted as part of the family instead of an interloper who stole ''her girl's'' affection and usurped Angel's place in bed.

Depending on the dog, however, changes are not always traumatic. Melanie says her Beagle, Precious, at seventeen has seen family births, celebrations, birthdays, graduations and weddings. Precious was a gift for Melanie's tenth birthday and now lives with Melanie, her husband and Ben, a Cocker Spaniel. Precious has accepted a new home, a new person and a new dog in her life with aplomb, probably because the little Beagle was included in all family activities.

Preparation is always the key word when dealing with pets. Explanation won't do any good. It's like speaking Greek to a two-year-old child. There's no hope they'll learn the language in time to be able to cope. If it is suddenly thrust on them, they simply can't understand a new husband, job demands or a divorce that throws everything into an uproar and changes their nice, comfortable life. This is especially true of older pets.

Youth is flexible. While a young dog might go with the flow and even learn how to swim upstream, an oldster prefers to bask in the sunshine, maybe do a little dog paddle now and then.

Foresight means not only calling the neighbor, Ms. Jones, to feed and walk Fluffy when you're delayed at work, but making sure Fluffy knows Ms. Jones and likes her. (It's also crucial to ascertain that Ms. Jones gets along with Fluffy and is always home at 6:00 P.M.) It means acclimating Fluffy to a crate and to being boarded—even if you never, ever use a crate, and even if you always take Fluffy along on trips. The time may come when these things become necessary.

Whether acquiring an older dog or preparing ours for the possibility of change, the most important time is now. Although we can't throw out our own life preserver, we can prepare for a disaster or minor upset beforehand. Preparation may be our pet's life preserver.

3

New Tricks

When you have an old dog,
you learn that old age
isn't so bad.
SIDNEY JEANNE SEWARD

$\mathbf{T}$HE HARDEST THING about retirement is that after they give you a gold watch and a pat on the back, they turn you out to pasture. As dogs grow older, we often treat them the same way—minus the gold watch.

A fertile brain grows dull with nothing but grass to mulch . . . or a chewbone to munch. A trim, fit body becomes soft and flabby when we do nothing but lie around, making us old before our time. There's nothing to look forward to or to be excited about. Anticipation stirs up the blood and starts us moving, and that's important. It keeps us in shape.

The alert dog owner watches for danger signs such as boredom and depression. A dog who used to dance with enthusiasm at the rattle of car keys will barely lift its head when all it means is being left home alone. Pacing, whining, lack of energy or licking at paws or legs are symptoms of stress. If a physical shows your dog is OK, give your dog a job to do or play a game and watch those warning signs recede. A simple job such as keeping a new kitten in line or teaching a younger

Norwich Terrier CH Thrumpton's Lord Timberson on his fifteenth birthday after a long walk in the woods with his children, grandchildren and great-grandchildren—tranquil, but filled with the self-assurance that only comes with wisdom and old age. Owners: Margaretta Wood and Johan Ostrow.

Ten-year-old Cairn Terrier U-UD Bonnie Bess UDT, TDI begging for her after-track goodie from owner Adel Swainston.

CH Eastern Waters' Oak CD, TD, WD, at age 10, capturing Best of Breed from the Veterans class at the National Specialty. Owners: Mr. and Mrs. Rupert J. Humer.

dog the rules of household etiquette seems to make the years melt away.

The active dog, like the active person, remains young in heart and spirit. Lying around doing nothing makes for a boring existence and gives us too much time to concentrate on our aches and pains. Modern psychology has taught us that those who stay busy have fuller, longer and, certainly, happier lives.

Too many of us are forced into retirement, making room for the youngsters, while we're still in our prime, and that can be true of our dogs also. We can choose to make their golden years a happy retirement instead of one dull day after another.

Bessie, a Cairn Terrier, is typical of an active dog that keeps busy. At ten, Bessie still loves to track. Adele, her owner, has shortened the official TDX track a bit. One day Adele indulged Bess and allowed her to track 375 yards twice—through water-filled ditches, over roads, through brush, around trees. Bess identified four articles and "finished the track soaking wet but happy." She is also a member of a pet therapy group, which allows her to perform her favorite tricks and obedience exercises at least once a week.

Athletic owners often run with their dogs, providing exercise for their pets and themselves at the same time. Marie's ten-year-old, eight-pound Toy Poodle accompanies her when she jogs. Marie says that Brandy has no idea she's a senior citizen.

The key in keeping up this type of strenuous activity is common sense. Watch for any change. If your pet begins to lag or seems to enjoy the activity less, it may be time to quit, slow down or substitute a less physically demanding task. As long as your vet and your dog's attitude give a thumbs up, chronological age is not important. Tom's Terrier mix, Dusty, ran with him for sixteen years, every day, and as far as twenty miles when he was training for a marathon.

A dog who can no longer run marathons with the family speedster can take a brisk walk with one of the slower humans in the household. Whenever someone goes for a walk, he or she can make a special point to take the family dog along. It's delightful to stroll in the woods or a park with a special friend. Just having the dog accompany you to the mailbox or around the block may be plenty. Excursions such as hiking, backpacking or swimming do not have to be curtailed if it's been done previously, and if the dog is feeling good and the weather is pleasant.

Just as we need to warm up before exercise, extra care must be taken of the canine athlete. Start and end with a walk; don't immedi-

Penny, age 11, the San Francisco SOCA Hearing Dog Program mascot.   *Peggy Parks*

At age 14, St. Hubert Giralda's mascot, Ding-A-Ling, visits a nursing home resident. Owner: St. Hubert's Giralda.

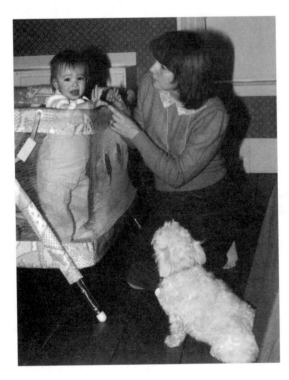

Hearing Ear Dog Molly Malone, age 10, alerts to a crying baby.

ately break into a run. Check your pet's feet and keep nails short. If there is ice or snow on the path, the dog might be more comfortable with doggy boots. High or low temperatures can affect a dog more quickly than we are aware. Your dog, in an effort to please you, might overdo if you don't say "Enough."

Sometimes, simply accompanying much-loved people to places where the dog can socialize is enough to give the dog an interest in life.

Whether large or small, a mission in life is important. St. Hubert's Giralda in Madison, New Jersey, is an organization dedicated to animal welfare. Ding A. Ling served as the mascot for St. Hubert's Giralda for ten years, greeting visitors to the estate and accompanying the staff to schools for humane education programs. Eventually the Pekingese became the first of the program's therapy dogs. She also served as official greeter for a time at the Dog Museum. Now officially retired at fourteen, Ling serves St. Hubert's in an "unofficial" capacity. The staff estimates she has been petted by at least 130,000 people.

That's the nice thing about a dog, no matter how often they're stroked, they never wear out. And they often make people forget their own troubles.

Working dogs, such as those trained to assist the disabled, willingly serve until they are no longer able to do so, whether that day comes early or late in life. Dog guides who lead those with visual problems or hearing dogs who alert their deaf owners to smoke alarms, crying babies or stove timers are more than a pet to their owners. They have a job to do, serving as a vital link to the rest of the world. A person who is confined to a wheelchair and who depends on a dog to open a swinging door or to carry schoolbooks does more than "just" love the dog. The dog is needed. It's nice to be needed.

Penny was rescued from the San Francisco SPCA to be a "test pilot" for a hearing dog program. Penny was so good, she became the demo dog for the project for the next eleven years. The program's staff say Penny has shown that shelter dogs can reach their full potential. They also say that Penny's worth a million dollars.

Sheep and cattle dogs often work willingly into their senior years. Police and defense dogs serve on the line as long as possible, then might be switched to a less demanding chore such as drug or bomb detection through scent work.

Unlike air-headed puppies, older dogs are sensitive to the needs of their masters and respond well to training or, if need be, even train themselves! More than one dog has compensated for its owner's vision or hearing loss with no formal training.

Once a skill is learned, dogs seldom lose their satisfaction in accomplishing a task. As they age, dogs can still experience the joy of doing their jobs and receiving their just rewards, even if the task is scaled back. Herding dogs can walk behind the sheep for the last few yards, for instance, instead of all the way from the far pasture.

Susan Butcher, multiple winner of the Iditarod, honored her old sled dog by letting him once again take the lead position on the team just before they crossed the finish line. Victory is sweet and so is applause—but the sweetest of all is seeing the joy on an old friend's face.

Serious fanciers are able to take advantage of club events and performances as well as tests. Many of these, such as Obedience demonstrations or Agility tests, allow dogs to perform at their own rate. The American Temperament Test Society certifies the dogs who react appropriately to various situations, such as loud noises and the approach of a stranger who suddenly opens an umbrella. Schoene, a German Shepherd, was nearly thirteen when she and her owner, Sharon, entered and passed. In 1989 the AKC approved a Canine Good Citizenship test, which opens a new field for many a well-behaved senior citizen as well as youngsters.

A German Shorthaired Pointer entered the Canine Good Citizen test and qualified at the age of fifteen. Winston's owner, Donna, says, "He was the oldest dog to qualify that day. He had a ball. He was so excited to go with the pups to a dog show again. His old gray face actually looked like he was smiling all day long. It's so nice to be able to do something with an old dog."

Even if you've never participated in the arena of dog shows, joining a dog club or a training class may be just what you and your pal need for rejuvenation.

Ginger had been a loyal pet and playmate to Karen's three small children for seven years. Then the oldest, Deanna, decided to join a 4-H dog training project with the Irish Setter. Karen says, "The two sulked and snitted at each other for the first year. Then at the state fair they somehow got it together to take a second-place ribbon in a large showmanship class. The following year their obedience started to gel as well."

When Ginger was ten, they entered their first AKC trial. "At one particularly hot trial, Ginger camped out under the judge's table dur-

ing the off lead heel exercise while her handler heeled around the ring alone. The judge told my daughter, 'Honey, I think she's just too old!' '' Ginger's CD was finished under that same judge when Ginger was eleven.

Because Ginger was still active, Karen began her in tracking and Ginger gained her Tracking Dog title at the age of fourteen. Deanna enjoyed her new hobby so much, she began training another dog when Ginger finished her first title.

Whether or not the owner intends to participate in formal events, a class encourages a dog/handler team to practice together at home and, hence, creates more togetherness.

The trainer thought Brooks would be too set in her ways and that J.M. would not be as firm with the old Lab as necessary. But J.M. thought Brooks would have fun in the class because she was so social. "What we hadn't counted on, any of us, was her willingness to do anything for me. Since she'd begun to show her eleven-plus years, I'd been reducing my expectations of her. But Brooks has gamely stayed with the hour program for the past nine weeks. She has learned to heel, and beautifully, to sit-stay and down-stay (that's the easiest one) and also to stand-stay, even as her leg trembles, struggling to hold the position until the trainer comes by to finish the exercise. Sometimes she makes it; sometimes she doesn't. She definitely tries. Heart."

One who is unable to compete with the young sprouts in the conformation ring can hold his own with any age in obedience. Both conformation shows and Obedience Trials offer classes for veterans, although some owners take their chances in the regular classes.

OLD DOGS—OLD TRICKS

Marijane had already showed her Sheltie, Nonnie, through her Utility Dog (UD) when Nonnie began exhibiting the consequences of former injuries. Nonnie enjoyed obedience so much, however, that Marijane was able to show in UKC with lower jumps and attain the UKC-CDX on her. Nonnie won all first placements in her U-CDX quest, plus a High in Trial award.

Mary is a firm believer of utilizing obedience training. Mary has learned a lot from her old dog. *"Charlie has taught me not to ignore him because of his age or to overlook his need for equal time and attention."*

U-CDX Nonnie CDX, at age 12.
Owner: Marijane Craig.
Santacroce's Photo Studio

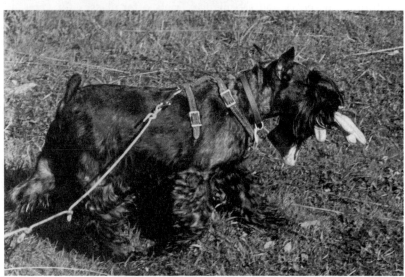

Ten-year-old Miniature Schnauzer BJ, TD, on the track. Owner: Betty J. Blake.

Am/Can CH U-HRCH UD Heron Acres Sandcastle MH UDTX, WCX, NAHRA MHR completed her Hunting title at age 10. Owner: Betty Drobac. *Schobel Photograph*

Mary believes that obedience is no good unless it is used. She usually dropped a few pairs of socks carrying the laundry upstairs, so, she says, "I decided to put Charlie's UD to work. I lined up the numerous pairs of rolled socks on a bench and let Charlie bring them upstairs for me. He delivers one pair at a time, then returns as fast as possible to retrieve another pair."

When Mary retired, she devoted her time to training her younger Weimaraner for a Novice Retrieving Dog (NRD) title. She says she concentrated her efforts on her younger dog, but Charlie would not be denied. "It broke my heart to leave Charlie at home.

"Last fall we were practicing with Diesel for the coming hunting tests when someone said they would like to see what old Charlie could do. He impressed us all with his ability. (No one ever doubted his desire.) He took off in the backfield as if he had wings, found game, pointed the bird and held point until the bird was flushed. This was his very first exposure to any kind of field work. He would have won his SD [Shooting Dog] soon after, but the gun failed to go off, so he didn't qualify. We plan to try again this fall. He made us very proud in the Retrieving ratings. At the present time we are working on tracking."

Substituting a "find the carrot" exercise instead of "find the bird" or "track" encourages your senior citizen to continue using his nose around the home. He receives a crunchy veggie as well as your praise for reward.

An eleven-year-old Borzoi with a spinal condition can't do some things anymore. But one thing she could still do, and loved, was track. So Linda humored her friend by entering her at a test. In the midst of the track, the judges began blowing their whistles, then blasting on them, then yelling. Linda and her dog had been concentrating so hard, they hadn't even noticed a man "flashing" in the midst of the track! The old girl seemed disgusted. Someone had ruined her fun.

When the judges offered them another try, Linda was perplexed. It was a lot to ask of the old gal, but she decided to give it a try. This time Carla finished her track undistracted, and there wasn't a dry eye in the gallery.

Nobody could say that Betty's Golden, Sandcastle, wasn't versatile. She had her American/Canadian Championship and her American/Canadian UDTX. Betty and Cassie had so enjoyed working together that when Betty heard about the Hunting Retriever Tests when Cassie was nine, she determined to try although neither of them had

U-UD, Can. OTCH Mo's Superstar Am CDX, TT, VB, herding sheep at age 11. Owner: Monika Hole.

Kahlua jumps through the hoop in an agility course. Kahlua was rescued from a trash bin twelve years before. Owner: Judi Schott.

ever been hunting. At their first practice, "We had a ball, watching and trying to imitate dogs that knew how to swing to the gun, quarter ahead of the handler yet be steady to wing and shot. In days to come, the latter was the hardest of all new things for Cassie to master. Nearly always sensibly steady on the field trial line, she turned into an un-disciplined Derby dog when the birds flushed unexpectedly under her nose. I couldn't help but enjoy her enthusiasm even as we worked hard for control."

They persevered and traveled from Michigan to the East Coast to attain Cassie's Master Hunter (MH). Now Cassie greets guests with two tennis balls in her mouth, inviting them to play.

OLD DOGS—NEW TRICKS AND OLD TRICKS

Agility courses test the dog's ability and willingness to face various obstacles. Darting through a tunnel, scaling a wall, walking across a ladder or jumping a brook are challenges your dog may never see in everyday life. Running up one side of a seesaw, balancing in the middle and dashing down the other end isn't something that either of you is likely to have to do—but it's fun! And the best part about agility is that it's just as much fun if the dog makes mistakes. At an informal introduction to agility, who cares if your old dogs do it right or how fast. If they enjoy it, do it.

Terriers, Herding dogs, sighthounds and hunting dogs all can participate in instinct tests. Terrier clubs hold digs where the dogs "go to the ground," zooming through a buried tunnel to reach the caged quarry at the end. The AKC's preliminary herding test shows whether the dog has the instinct of its ancestors, and the field tests demonstrate a hunting dog's birdiness. Chasing a dummy in a lure coursing event evokes the ancient urges of the sighthounds.

All of these are held in a controlled environment with experienced testers, so that a dog with some infirmities won't become lost, confused or allowed to do more than is wise. People welcome situations where their old Bouvier can contentedly herd a couple of docile ducks or their Pointer can once again freeze into a proud stance over a planted pheasant. (Note: Blind or lame dogs may not compete in AKC events.)

When the herding instinct tests began, Ted took a seat on the hill with his thirteen-year-old Bearded Collie, Bridget. She had cataracts, as well as arthritis. She was too old to be entered in the test, but Ted thought she'd enjoy being out with the other dogs and their owners. Bridget paid close attention to the ducks and seemed almost to "Tsk, tsk" when a youngster seemed disinterested in the stock. Finally she could stand it no longer and darted away from Ted, neatly rounding up and gathering the ducks together. Bridget did such a good job that later she was called in to round them up again and was awarded her Herding Certified (HC) from the Bearded Collie Club of America.

At another herding test, Jeff thought it would be fun to test their aging Belgian Tervuren, Riot, even though he himself didn't know how to direct the dog. Riot did a great job and Jeff was extremely proud until he suddenly noticed thirty sheep thundering directly at him at a dead run with Riot bringing the sheep "home" as his instinct told him. Jeff's instinct was to bolt toward the fence and dive over—which he did. Riot received his Herding Trial Championship at the age of nine.

Veterans of the hunt rarely forget their lust for the sport. Sonny, a Brittany with an illustrious background (Am/Can/Bahama CH), still loves to sniff out birds despite arthritis. Because he's nearly deaf, his owner, Barbara, is careful to hunt him only in fenced fields. But when he's in the field, she says he becomes young again.

Charles says that his old dogs, from eight years on, showed their best years in the field. Maybe that's because Charles's dogs "have always been treated like my kids except for college and driver's training." One of his dogs, at the age of twelve, tried to catch salmon in the shallow, but swift, portions of streams in Alaska. Charles had to quit hunting moose, deer and antelope because his dog wouldn't let him out of the house with any gun unless he went along. Old habits die hard.

It's wonderful to be able to satisfy a desire that great. So wonderful that even when owners know the excursion may be debilitating physically, they often grant the dog a last hunt. They take pictures to remember the occasion—a field, the dog and a bird on a warm day—with yet warmer tears burning as the owners recall a time when they and the dog had a lifetime to build memories. Now the most important picture is the one taken with the heart. Another Brittany owner wrote, "What she loved most was hunting. . . . It was even more painful to decide not to hunt Queenie than it was to make the eventual decision to end her life."

Am/Can/Bda CH Wincrest Number One Son, a top show Brittany, is still keen for the hunt at age 12. Sonny's excursions are carefully controlled due to his hearing loss. Owner: Barbara Scott.

U-CDX CH Sierra Sch-Roo Sabu UD, TT, TDI, age 7, crosses the catwalk obstacle in the Agility course. Owner: Jacqueline Root.

Heron Acres Meadowpond Gofer CD, JH, WC went for her titles at age 9 in order to qualify her dam as an Outstanding Dam. Owner: Betty Drobac.

Honey Sweet Golden Emily CD, WC attained her field title at the age of 10. Owner: Melissa Goodman, DVM.

Such enthusiasm is favored by dog owners, and the dogs who have it are special. Some are a mite spoiled.

Old Mary was known for her rabbit tracking ability for counties around. She always rode in the truck cab with Ron on the way to the hunt. But one day when Ron's friend Bill picked them up, Bill said there wasn't any room up front in his new truck, so Old Mary would have to ride in the dog box with the others. Well, Old Mary's famous nose was out of joint, and she didn't live up to her reputation that day, for she sat sulking under the truck while the others hunted. Bill said next time he'd ride in the dog box so Old Mary could have her usual place on the seat.

Her talents made her popular, and the duo were in demand for hunting expeditions. Old Mary was the center of attention wherever they went, and Ron was her chauffeur. While she showed off for the other hunters and basked in her glory, Ron stood by and proudly grinned.

But it wasn't long before Ron's nose was the one out of joint, and it was the old Basset Hound's fault. It happened one day when Bill called up and asked Ron to come over and bring Old Mary. Ron explained that Mary was expecting pups and couldn't come along. He hung up the phone with an abashed look.

"What's wrong?" Ron's wife, Barb, asked.

"Well," Ron answered, "Bill said we could just make it some other time. It was really Old Mary he wanted."

That special instinct can survive lulls and detours. Don't assume it's too late.

Flying Dutchman Von Rip Traf, a German Shorthaired Pointer, was within two field trial points of attaining his Dual Championship when his owner, George, took a two-year hiatus from competition. But when Dutch was ten, the duo came back and beat twenty-four of the top field dogs to finish the coveted Dual title.

With a bit of training, it's not too hard to encourage your dog to use his instincts in another arena. Although dogs are born knowing how to follow their noses, sometimes it takes the owners a bit longer to point those talented sniffers toward a goal. Nevertheless, one Chesapeake Bay Retriever earned his TD (Tracking Dog) title at the age of twelve, the oldest at that time. Today, even older dogs attempt and pass tracking.

Many owners find tracking something dogs can do after putting more strenuous sports behind them.

CH/OTCH Rhydowen Fy Flaen Llwynogn heeling happily beside owner Carli Bates. At age 12 "Foxi" was still in the top ten obedience Cardigan Welsh Corgis.

After Niki, a Siberian Husky, retired from sled-dog racing, he attained a UD (Utility Dog) title at the age of nine. His owner, Lori, then decided to give him a try at tracking, which was less physically demanding. At eleven, Niki attained his TD. That day a judge remarked, "There's one dog out there who should be a TDX [Tracking Dog Excellent]—the Siberian." So, of course, there was only one thing to do.

Niki was almost thirteen when they entered their first TDX test. Lori admits she blew the first one, and a strong wind blew the second. Before Niki's next chance, it became necessary to have surgery to remove a tumor on his leg. Lori says he permanently lost feeling in two toes, along with a summer's worth of tracking. But just a month short of Niki's fourteenth birthday, they gave it another try.

Lori says of that moment, "I doubt that there was anyone watching that day who hadn't heard about how old Niki was, or what was at stake that day; the support for him was fantastic. And this time Niki didn't stand and sniff the breeze—he was tracking even before he reached the starting flag. He hesitated briefly at the first turn, then took off with me running at the end of his forty-foot line. He slowed down only slightly for the articles and didn't appear to notice crosstracks. Not even two consecutive six-foot ravines at about 900 yards slowed him down, although he did glance back to be sure I was coming. Everything went so quickly I didn't realize we were at the final article until I looked back and saw one of the judges running up, waving his arms and yelling, 'Congratulations!' Niki had run the track in just ten minutes and five seconds—an incredible time, even for a young dog. Amid the congratulations, there were many tears of joy that day. Niki had just become the first Siberian Husky TDX, the first Siberian UDTX and the oldest dog of any breed to pass a TDX test. Niki was happy too. He ran through the field and back to the car for a treat."

At age sixteen, Niki died and was buried with his TDX glove.

Dogs love to work and, even more, to please you. Whoever came up with the saying that you can't teach an old dog new tricks was never loved by an old dog. Throughout their long lives, even without training, these veterans have picked up a lot more than we realize.

Here she is in an obedience class receiving praise for things she's been doing for years. *Sit, you say? Hey, easy, I learned that as a pup for treats. Heel? Who wants to run ahead anyway? Come? Well, of course, I'll come! This is my favorite person in my whole world.*

That joy of working with their owners must seem like play to the

Nikolai iz Taiga UDTX, tracking at age 14. Owner: Terry and Lori Plampin.

Sabu, age 7, and Trella UD TDI, age 8, are working Therapy Dogs. Owner: Jackie Root.

Puffy Cloud of Golden CDX, age 11, herds sheep instead of reindeer. Owners: Terry and Lori Plampin.
Kent and Donna Dannen

Italian Greyhound Colacove Day Dream UDT working the Utility articles at age 8.
Owner: Karen M. Froemming.

dogs, and if they're not invited due to their advanced years, they'll crash the party.

Pat's Missy hadn't done any obedience since she was six. She was fourteen when Pat brought some jumps for another dog. Pat says, "Missy stood in front of them and kept barking so my other dog couldn't jump. I put the jump down to an eight-inch board, and she jumped over and back a few times. Missy thought this was the greatest thing."

It seems they never forget. On the other extreme, Helen didn't start her German Shorthaired Pointer, Geoff, until a friend suggested they attend obedience classes together when Geoff was six. Six months later, Geoff had his CD (Companion Dog). They enjoyed it so much they went on even though Helen thought the jumping made the CDX (Companion Dog Excellent) an elusive "long shot." A year later, Geoff had his CDX. She says, "I kept thinking I shouldn't be asking Geoff to do all the jumping needed for training. But Geoff didn't know he was getting old—he jumped effortlessly. So I decided we'd go ahead and train for Utility. I thought we'd stop when he got too old to jump." Geoff earned his UD four months short of his eleventh birthday. She says, "I sure am glad I didn't think my dog was too old to learn anything."

Geoff was retired before he realized he was "supposed to be too old." But it doesn't always happen that way. How *do* you know when to retire a dog?

Lori had another dog at the same time as Niki. As a youngster, Puffy, a Samoyed, enjoyed sled-dog racing and made his mark in the world of weight pulling by setting a state record in Colorado. When he retired from that, Lori decided to head back to the obedience ring with Puff. He was seven when he made his CDX. Lori started Utility training when Puff was nine.

She says, "He entered his first show when he was nine and a half. He knew the exercises, but his goal was not a qualifying performance. He was out to enjoy himself and to please the audiences he loves so well."

She says he never qualified, always erring in a new, comedic way. "He just hated being bored! After failing Puff for trying to squeeze out through a hole in the baby gate, a sympathetic judge consoled me, 'I'm sure he'll settle down in a year or two.' When I informed her that he was ten and a half, she could only sigh, 'Oh, dear.' "

Lori worried whether she would know when to retire him, but "Puffy told me when he was ready to quit. When he was eleven years

CH Happiness is Elegance CDX taking the high jump at age 7. Owner: Susan Rowe.

Peg Nita

Giant Schnauzer, CH BN's Razz Beri Jo Bair K CDX TD PCE, Can. CD TD TDI, age 7, is also a working Rescue dog. Owner: Betty Blake.

old, at a show with excellent footing, Puffy ran to the correct jump, then stopped and looked straight at me. (When he blew an exercise, he never looked at me.) When he did it for both jumps, my decision was made. We pulled from the next day's show, and I never asked him to jump again. I had always thought it would be very difficult to retire an obedience dog without the title I had worked so hard to obtain. But it wasn't hard to stop showing Puffy. We had both totally enjoyed all the shows we entered and never left the ring without a smile."

When he died, a little neighborhood child who disliked most dogs cried when she told her mother, "Mommy, I don't like dogs, but I loved Puffy!"

Some dogs continue their activity into old age, while others don't begin until they're older, like the Norwich Terrier who attended his first dog show at the age of eleven and finished with three five-point majors. And then there's Dolores's Lhasa Apso, Penny, who became C Mysta Thruppence finally at the lofty age of eleven after working toward that goal at various intervals over her entire life. Neither one of that partnership gave up.

Sarah, a Cairn Terrier, already an American Champion, completed her Canadian Championship at the age of nine years at a Terrier specialty, competing against her own grandchildren and great-grand children, as well as thirteen other females less than half her age. Her proud owner, Glenn, says that "Sarah truly deserved her win, having sound movement and great coat. Before Sarah's breeder died, I promised she would finish her Championship, and she did in grand style."

Sarah keeps Glenn hopping. She has learned to open bi-fold doors to the food storage. Her passion is cookies. In her various forages, she chewed open the top of a container of olive oil, giving all the dogs a treat (as well as diarrhea); the next week they had popcorn kernels (and a trip to the vet). When a bag of sand was placed over her beloved cookies, she dug a hole through the bag into the cookies. Glenn groaned at the sand everywhere, but one can imagine the grin as he admits, "But, oh, how I love her."

At the venerable age of fourteen and a half, Baron, a Schipperke, captured Best of Opposite Sex at the breed's National Specialty Show.

His owner, Tish, said in her tribute to "Old Mannie: Veteran Schipperke,"* "What creates a dog of this caliber and maintains the

* Pure-Bred Dogs/American Kennel Gazette, June 1987.

Nine-year-old U-CDX Spartan's Sampson CD, TT, TDI, an American Staffordshire Terrier, conquers an Agility obstacle. Samson is a popular registered Therapy Dog. Owner: Virginia Isaac.

Veteran Komondor CH Gillian's A Kodiak Bear CDX, Can. CD flies over the jump with ease. Kody finished the Canadian UD at age 11. Owners: John D. Landis and Barbara Artim.

Molly says hard to port, Schnitzel says hard to starboard. Mary Lu says full speed ahead. Owner: Mary Lu Rang.

creation? Three things, I think. Primarily, the breeder, who puts all of the genes together and is responsible for the appearance of the dog. Secondly, the love given by the [co-]owner(s) and then by me gave him the feeling that he really was something special. Last of all, and possibly the most important, is the God-given gift of heart. Is it there at birth? Is it developed? I don't know. But when it is present in either man or beast, it's a glory to behold. I do know my bear-dog had an abundance of it."

She describes Baron's win at the Schipperke Club of America. "I was proud of him. He was in magnificent condition with no obvious old-age infirmities, and I wanted others to see this.

"There were no expectations of winning. When I saw the lineup in the Veterans class with some of the 'Who's Who' guys still being shown, I thought Baron would be lucky to be awarded even a placement. It was a very warm day and I worried that my old boy lacked the stamina to withstand the temps. I was fully prepared to pick him up at the first sign of stress and ask to be excused.

"My heart almost burst with pride when I put Baron down on the mat and he immediately flew to the end of the six-foot lead. Show dog again! From that moment on, he was the darling of the crowd and there was vigorous applause each time he was moved. The love and admiration I felt for this marvelous animal as the competition continued cannot be described and would not have been diminished if he had not won a single ribbon. The tears never cleared from my eyes."

If the show ring isn't your thing, or your dog's, or it is but a pleasant memory, that doesn't mean you both should sit and gather moss. Whatever it takes to bring back that youthful enthusiasm, strengthen the bond between the two of you and put a glint in your old guy or gal's eyes, do it.

Old and young dogs alike also love to play with Nyladiscs and Frisbees. As the dog slows down or arthritis becomes a problem, the game can still be pursued by bending the rules a bit. Throw the disc a little slower or roll it along the ground. The object isn't to launch your dog into orbit but to end the game with a warm feeling in your heart—not one that requires Ben-Gay.

Jason loved to play Frisbee. He was able to jump as high as three feet to grab the disc and did so until he was more than twelve years old. This passion to jump caused complications, however, when Marion began to train her other dog, Hutch, for his CD. Jason and Hutch were such buddies that Jason, a mixed breed, insisted on training alongside the Golden Retriever. When Hutch attained his CD, he began further training with jumps. There was Jason jumping in tandem.

Although Jason loved to jump, Hutch did it because he had to. Hutch preferred lying in the sun and watching airplanes fly from one end of the sky to the other. Their togetherness continued throughout their lives. They died just three weeks apart.

Like Hutch, some dogs prefer a slower pace while still remaining alert and active. It's not the speed of the pace, it's being together. Being with that most important person is a vital part of all canine activities. Whether it's jogging, soccer, showing, playing or working, it's fun when you're with someone you love.

When Mary Lu goes boating, eleven-year-old Molly accompanies her . . . provided Molly can sit in the front of the boat and play captain. While on the boat, Molly keeps tabs on Schnitzel, who is only six years old. The old Schnauzer has her own life jacket and a busy social life. Mary Lu says, "Between Molly's commanding presence in the boat and her life vest, she attracts quite a bit of attention from landlubbers and other sailors. Even wildlife such as deer, beaver and ducks pay their respects to the little boat's commander. Frequently people in other boats will row over to say hello. Molly always enjoys making new friends."

That's what it's all about: making new friends while keeping the old. Dogs are social creatures and, although they often have a special feeling bordering on adoration that belongs to only one person or one family, most welcome the attention of other people. Social butterflies, even canine ones, rarely become hermits as they age unless it's forced upon them. Taking them with you on errands or visiting friends is a perfect excuse to be together.

4

Steady As She Goes

*Forsake not an old friend; for the new is not
comparable to him: A new friend is as new wine;
when it is old, thou shalt drink it with pleasure.*
ECCLESIASTES 9:10

As WE AGE, we grow more and more resistant to change. Anything new is looked upon with suspicion because the status quo is so comfortable. We've arranged our lives the way we like them, we want to keep them that way, and that's that.

We've even learned to accept necessary irritants like taking out the garbage or paying our taxes. Our lives have reached the point where we'd miss doing these chores if we didn't have to do them. It's like waking up with an itch every morning. If the itch disappears, we still have the urge to scratch.

When we are very young, time moves slowly. It seems forever before our birthday or a holiday arrives. As we grow older, the days seem to pass more quickly and finally they're speeding by. We look in the rearview mirror and see the miles behind us. Suddenly we notice that we're no longer young. We may feel the same, but the years have left their mark.

As we struggle against the swiftly moving current, we are determined to mark time and tread water. We become accustomed to a

Saruman, a 19-year-old Kuvasz. Owner: Edward Freeman.

Happy, at age 10, is typical of his breed, still looking forward to a romp in the snow. Owner: Michelle Gamblin.

certain pattern in our lives, and so it is with our dogs. If you've always fed Fidelity at precisely 5:30 P.M., you can set your watch by her sitting at the feeding station and looking espectantly at you. As our dogs age, we want to keep life as comfortable and comforting as possible. One way we can do that is to follow an established routine— make necessary changes gradually and minimize stress.

It doesn't take much effort to fulfill simple desires. Michelle says her Brittany, Freckles, still loves to chase butterflies. Ray's old Shepherd, Baron, always plays with a red ball, and Jerry's Whippet, Silky, has to check out the bottom of his grocery bags every time, "just to make sure I didn't leave anything good in them."

Happiness comes in different forms and sometimes that means work, or at least a pretense of such. Owners of working animals allow them to perform self-imposed chores simply because it makes them happy.

Edward rescued a Kuvasz who had followed his guarding instincts. The resulting bite brought a death sentence, commuted when Edward offered to take Saruman to his large country kennel. The dog spent the rest of his life guarding their home and several acres. Saruman loved to wander about the property, and his owners couldn't deny him that even as he began to show his advanced age.

Edward recalls, "In his nineteenth year, Saruman was getting frail and showed stiffness from arthritis. His eyesight was very good. He didn't appear to be deaf. He still could go hunting down a couple miles in the valley on his bush trails. He would stay out till dark when we would drive down and pick him up. We would find him sitting and looking over the valley, listening and waiting, playing the role of the mighty predator. When he saw us, he would happily allow us to lift him into the vehicle and head for home contented and relaxed."

Although many senses grow faint with progressing age, one thing that seems to increase as we grow older is our love of a good meal, despite the fact that we are often less active and need less food. As each year passes, it is common to find ourselves liking more and more foods. Our list of dislikes grows shorter. Some seniors josh that eating is one of the fun things left in life. Dinner may be the highlight of the day for your elderly dogs—next to you, their favorite thing is food.

Although a healthy diet is necessary, we can make dinner a pleasurable experience. Just as we set a pretty table or whip up a luscious recipe for ourselves, so we can cater to our pets' whims.

If she's used to eating at 5:30 P.M., punch that time clock. Not

Zestee, CD, age 11, is called Granny by her owner Zona Munro, but still keeps sharp eyes and ears at mealtime.

Fred Hawkins, 10 years old, reclines in his sleeping bag. Owner: Rosemarie Hawkins.

OTCH Shoreland's Big Harry Deal achieved 1,321 OTCH points within one year at age 11, to become 1989's top Obedience Dog. Owner: Sue Mayborne.

only is it important for her sense of security and helps to prevent digestive upsets, but it may be vital with certain physical conditions, such as diabetes. If she's developing a bit of a paunch, use nonfattening, low-sodium fillers. Find a quality food she likes, then stick with it. Don't switch brands and think she needs variety just because we humans don't want to eat meatloaf every day. Fanny will take her Senior Chow Plus, with a bit of green beans on the top, every day promptly at seven o'clock, thank you.

Feed her in the same place and watch for changes in her appetite. If her eagerness fades or she begins to leave a little food, that's the time to make an appointment for a checkup. Following a healthy report, try cutting back a bit or offer two small snacks rather than one large meal. You might warm the food a bit or sprinkle a bit of garlic powder on top. Both are inducements for picky eaters. Soaking food to a mushy consistency or using a food processor to grind the large pieces finer makes it easier for the toothless dog to gum a meal. ''Funny,'' one owner remarked, ''I did this for Lemon when I weaned her and her litter from their mother. Now, thirteen years later, we've come full circle.''

Don't allow other pets too disturb Granny during dinner. Just because she's eating more slowly doesn't mean that Junior should scarf it down the moment her head is turned. If necessary, confine other pets until she's had her fill in peace.

Mealtimes are a logical reminder to give medications, another reason to be timely. Pills can be crushed and hidden in food or dosed separately with a dab of canned meat, liverwurst or another favorite, peanut butter.

Although meal size stays the same or even decreases, output seems to increase. One of the signs of advanced age is a more frequent need for outings. The bladder is like an old, tired balloon, saggy and thin-skinned. It won't hold as much and needs to be emptied more often. Your dog will be more comfortable with four or five short walks rather than two long ones each day. With decreased hearing and energy taking its toll, your old friend is likely to sleep deeply and may need to be awakened for regular excursions. Problems with incontinence are circumvented partially by increasing the number of potty breaks.

Even young dogs spend part of the day sleeping, and the temptation for catnaps increases with each passing year. Old gents saw wood in the middle of the day and don't bother to use the excuse that they're ''just resting their eyes.'' The canine senior needs the extra snooze time and should have a private place where he can snore peacefully without disturbance if he wishes. This is where the crate-trained dog has an advantage.

When Abby wants to take a nap, she goes to her den, which is located conveniently in a corner of the family room. It's the same crate she was housebroken in as a pup and where she was confined when she was left alone as a youngster. By the time she was dependable, she didn't want to give it up. It was her home within her family's home.

As the years passed, she went to her crate whenever she wanted to get away from hubbub and commotion. She even learned to open the door. Now that she's thirteen, she finds it comforting to take her naps in her own little house. No one disturbs her, but she's close to the action. She can join in when she wants.

People have various demands on their time that occasionally necessitate a late-night session sweating over a tax return or answering long-put-off correspondence. Now and then we enjoy staying up late to read a good book or watch a favorite movie on television. But old dogs like to rise and retire at the same time they always have. They couldn't care less if Bogart and Bacall are beckoning and are likely to show their displeasure at a break in the routine by nudging your arm or sighing at your feet. Some sit and stare at you, much as a disapproving in-law, until you feel guilty enough to give up and retire to the bedroom.

Some canine seniors are lazy and refuse to participate in activities and need to be coaxed or coerced into action. Although these cantankerous old folks can be trying, they're worth making the extra effort for.

Adam is Su's first old dog. She says, "While he tries my patience enormously, he warms my heart continuously." The thirteen-year-old mini Dachsie and Su "butt heads frequently on the subject of rules, and who makes them.

"Morning is Adam's least favorite time of day," Su comments. "He sleeps in my bed and the prospect of leaving his warm bed makes him scramble for the furthest nether regions."* After Su tears off the sheets and carries the complaining little guy down the stairs, he turns around and heads right back up—so now she carries him around the corner.

---

* "An Aging Dog Brings Changes and Special Memories," by Su Stout, *Dog Fancy*, July 1990, p. 67.

Missy, at age 12, never missed a chance to tell the mail carrier what she thought. Owner: Pat Slemmer.

Bonnie, age 11, and Bambie, age 7, heading out for their daily walk. Bonnie will not leave the house without her Snoopy toy. Owner: Loretta Ralph.

No matter how thick the dust of battle each morning, both are winners, enjoying the extra cuddle time together.

Exercise is always important, although it might change from strenuous to moderate to mild as the years pass. Not only is exercise a good way of keeping the body in shape, it also keeps the dog's attitude healthy.

If a dog is used to greeting neighbors on the daily walk or looks forward to a canine playtime in the park, we need to make sure that still happens. Even though we both walk slower and don't cover as much territory, or our pet will watch the youngsters from the security of a lap, the mental stimulation is much needed. If up to it, Spot can toddle after a ball or fetch an occasional stick.

Little things make up the whole, and it's these little things that matter when changes must be made. Even moving halfway across the country isn't so bad when you've still got your buddy, your toys and your din-din at the right time.

A familiar routine should be followed with as few deviations as possible. If you always take an after-breakfast walk, don't suddenly eliminate this pleasant outing together. Make it shorter or set your alarm earlier if you need to begin work at your usual walk time.

Dogs love to please their human family, which is why they never tire of performing the same trick over and over. If Harvey always jumps over a stick for his treat, lower the stick as needed—even if it has to be laid on the ground. He won't know the difference; he'll only know that jumping over the stick brings a goodie, not how high the stick is.

Each time Lee left the house, he told his young Mastiff to "watch the house," even though Lee knew Dirk was a pussycat and would probably kiss any would-be prowler to death. Homecoming was always a big deal. Lee praised Dirk for guarding the house and told him what a wonderful dog he was. It was as much a part of their day as getting up and going to bed. By the time Dirk was fourteen, he was nearly blind and would have to gum an intruder, but the command was always the same, "Watch the house, Dirk."

And the homecoming was the same too, full of joy and pride, wags and heartwarming thumps.

Old dogs, like old people, tend to cling to the familiar. Everything may be a bit dimmer—sight, sound and even smell. Staying at home isn't as frightening as going to a new place where things startle a dog whose senses are used to working in pastels instead of neon.

CH Southern Gentleman, CDX, a Mastiff, still qualified in obedience at 9½ years old. "Chopper" is the first male CH CDX Mastiff in the breed's history and is the constant companion of Lisa Nicolello.

Bryn's Magaera Am/Can UD, at age 12, is still top dog when she plays with Raquel Wolf. Owner: Mary D. Fine.

CH Gleanngay Holliday ROM, age 11, patiently waits for the pre-show grooming routine. Owner: Gay Sherman.

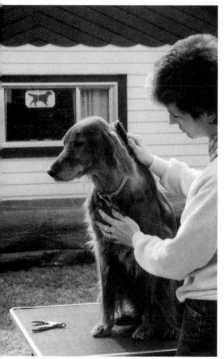

Barb Turek brushes her 11-year-old Irish Setter, Barb's Wish Upon a Star CD. "Maggie" looks forward to her weekly session.   *Kathy Cragg*

Carol and Max always boarded their Dachsies, Katie (fifteen) and Missy (sixteen), when they went on vacation. But then Katie developed Cushing's disease, losing her hair and much of her sight. Her owners were able to help Katie adjust with a whole wardrobe of T-shirts and sweaters to keep her warm, and they kept her on familiar turf to eliminate stress.

Now they hire a dog sitter when they travel. Someone stays overnight doling out love, attention, medication and food. The dogs don't have to cope with strange surroundings and aren't exposed to the germs that dwell in even the cleanest of kennels. They have their meals and exercise in their customary environment, enjoy socializing with the sitter at night and spend the day as usual, snoozing anywhere they wish.

Many dogs remain healthy, although less active, until the end of their lives. Having an undemanding pet becomes simple, so simple that it's easy to forget the old dog is there. One owner admits that she did.

All Francine's Miniature Pinschers rode along to training class. The pups bounced around greeting everyone, and the show dogs went through their paces. The older set were placed in a wire exercise pen to watch and gladly accept the pats as people passed by.

After the class, everyone romped and played for a bit, then were loaded up for the ride home—all except the fourteen-year-old who had fallen asleep under a tree. When the oversight was discovered, Francine made a sharp about-turn and found her old dog patiently waiting for her return. "Now we count noses," Francine said.

Quiet, undemanding dogs might be easy to overlook, and it's often easier to leave them behind than to take the time needed to include them in excursions. It takes longer to put on a harness than to slip on a collar. When everyone's lined up for a picture in front of the Christmas tree and Grandma decides to lie down, the lineup is not quite as perfect. But these are precious memories.

KEEPING UP APPEARANCES

Grooming becomes a job with little compensation and, therefore, a busy schedule makes it tempting to skip the oldster. No matter how much time owners or professional groomers spend, we can't make up for the thinner hair, looser skin and saggy back. Nails are thick and tough, seeming to grow even more quickly with less exercise to wear

A Saturday night bath is part of 13-year-old Buck's routine.   *Renée Stockdale*

them down. Teeth are worn and discolored. Mats appear overnight in long coats because the dog dribbles food and spends more time lying down. Hair tangles at pressure points: behind the elbow, under the groin, around the genitals, near the ears.

An old dog often objects to detangling, tooth scaling and a pedicure with yipes or jerking away a paw. Our hearts melt and we are tempted to give in to the protests. Yet a thorough grooming is just as necessary as when they were younger—perhaps more so since this serves as an in-home checkup. In addition, a vigorous brushing helps stimulate natural oils, which in turn aid dry skin and restore the luster of the coat. So we need to resist the temptation to stop bugging them and, instead, continue the session with patience and gentle handling, making the sessions shorter and less intense.

Because of the seniors' increased tendency to mat, some owners elect to clip or trim long coats on oldies, sacrificing glamour for their comfort. Scissor hair to a two-inch length instead of a floor drape, or try out a Schnauzer trim. It's surprising how dogs can shed years along with the hair. The pet's shorter hair can also make it easier for the owner to identify a problem otherwise hidden by thick tresses.

Old dogs enjoy the closeness and bonding that goes on during a grooming session, and this is another reason they should not be ignored because it's no longer necessary—or possible—for them to have their former glamour. Whether for a new crewcut or long, flowing locks, dogs love to hear how beautiful they are. One owner warned that someone laughed at her newly shorn Bearded Collie, and the dog spent a week hiding under the bed and pouting. Now whenever she clips the old gal down, she is careful to tell her, "Oh, you're soooo pretty, Breezy!" Breezy preens and struts just like she used to when her long brown locks shone and glistened after a bath and coiffure in preparation for a show.

When Tiny turned nine years old, Roxanne's groomer suggested that it would be less stressful for the old Poodle to eliminate the close trim on Tiny's feet. They decided to do her in a puppy clip. The coat was easier to maintain without pompoms, needed to be clipped less often and looked sprightly.

"The funny thing is, the first time we did it, Tiny zoomed around the shop two or three times, wagging her tail, bouncing up and down, acting like she did when she was a puppy. Now she does this every time. It's like Samson and Delilah, except when Tiny's hair is cut, she doesn't lose her strength—she loses her adult demeanor."

Roxanne added that as soon as they arrive home, Tiny brings her the leash so that she can prance around the neighborhood and show off her new "do."

Other owners wish to keep the long coat and conduct shorter sessions more frequently, brushing and combing gently. Mats can be cut out if necessary, and they should be removed before shampooing. When bathing the dog, use conditioners to aid in easier comb-outs. A human dandruff shampoo or one prescribed by the veterinarian helps those with dry, scaly skin. Thoroughly dry the old guy and keep him out of drafts.

Dogs that require professional grooming present a different sort of problem. Be sure to discuss the senior's health with the groomer, pointing out sores or warts that need to be avoided during clipping. If your pet is comforted by your presence, ask if you can stay during the session. A dog that is unable to stand for the entire time might need rest breaks while other dogs are groomed.

Regular brushing at home will help eliminate mats, thereby making a session at the groomer's shorter, less painful and less expensive as well. Ask the groomer to make suggestions for between-appointment care to make your pet more comfortable. Many groomers will clip the dog's tummy hair close and shave around the genitals for comfort and cleanliness.

To show off, tie a jaunty bandana around your dog's neck or buy a sport collar and go for a walk. You'll be surprised at the spring in Barry's step when he feels good and is told he looks good.

One of the oddities of human society is that we tend to avoid that which is unpleasant; thus, people tend to tiptoe around anyone exhibiting physical limitations or even extreme old age.

THE AGE OF RESPECT

Joan said that she hated telling people her Yorkie's age. As soon as she answered, "Twenty," their faces changed and they drew back from the little dog. "It's as though her ancient age brought them within sight of death. There's nothing I can do about Harlowe's age, but that doesn't mean that I'm going to stop enjoying every minute I have with her.

"It's difficult now to take a walk," Joan added. "All her doggie friends have died, the neighborhood kids have grown up and have kids

Buck, age 13, and his friend know that play is hard work for both young and old. *Renée Stockdale*

Lucas O'Lucky CD, at age 16, poses for the annual Christmas photo with his younger friends. Owner: Diana Behrend.
Photo by Paulette

CH Tails-West Tammy UD finishing her Utility degree at age 11. Tammy was number one Obedience Silky Terrier in 1982. Owner: Dorothy Huber.

of their own. Everyone waves briefly at me, then turns back to their own 'busyness,' ignoring Harlowe as though she were already gone.

"It's a shame that others are missing what she has to give. Her tail still wags, and she still welcomes a pat with a thankful kiss on their hand. I wonder if I could pass her off as twelve. . . ."

Excursions take more time and more planning. Steps are slower, stops are more frequent and sometimes it's necessary to carry a small dog partway. But the slower pace allows us more time to smell the roses, to talk to our dog, to sit on a park bench quietly stroking an old gray head.

When a walk, nursing home visit or obedience exercise is part of the routine, it means we set aside time to be with a special dog. These old guys are so uncomplaining and patient that it's easy to forget them or shove aside their time for "more important" tasks. Yet few things are more important than spending time with a friend.

We need to take a lesson from dogs themselves. They don't recognize they're aging. Even puppies don't shy away from a gray-beard. They seem to sense an aura that makes them respect the oldster, but that doesn't stop them from taking an invitation to play. And if the older dog feels like a romp and joins in, no admonitions about "acting your age" or "what will people think!"

Nevertheless, owners should supervise and avoid competition. Youth bests old age in most events that demand athletic prowess, and it's no fun to lose all the time. This is a good time to practice some obedience commands with the younger set. Put a pup on a "sit, stay," enforced by a leash, if necessary, while Gramps gets a head start to the ball.

Experience counts for a great deal, however, and an older dog can be a mentor for a younger one. A hunter can teach a youthful Pointer to honor the veteran's find. Obedience exercises can be taught in a brace. As the older dog performs well, praise is given and the younger one watches and learns. Sled-dog enthusiasts often put the most experienced dog in the lead or at the wheel, letting the trainees learn from doing. A working farm dog's experience and wisdom balances out the younger's enthusiasm and boundless energy.

Make sure the old guy isn't overwhelmed by a galloping herd of younger dogs. We don't want dog—or ego—injured by overly rough play.

For many years, Thor had been top dog and knew it. As time passed, he had relaxed his authority with most things, but he was still very bossy about being first out the door. The first time there was a confrontation with raised hackles, Amy knew what caused it. Thor's son, Blitz, had taken charge and ruled the troops. That was fine as long as Thor allowed it, but when he protested, Amy realized it would be Thor who lost if a scuffle took place. So Amy takes care to avoid face-to-face combat. Whenever the two dogs go out together, she puts Blitz on a leash and a "sit, stay" until Thor has safely and sedately exited.

PRIVILEGES

A houseful of dogs and people should be like a heart. No matter how many are in it, a special corner should always be reserved for a special dog.

As noted, the senior dog has earned the place as top dog and deserves certain privileges, but that doesn't give license to disobey household rules. Rules are meant to be broken, but that's by bending them ourselves, not by our dogs doing so. Sometimes age brings stubbornness and a tendency to ignore authority. Although we might secretly admire the heart in the old dog, there are certain things that must be done and enforced whether or not they like it.

People often complain jokingly that their dogs or kids (or sometimes spouses) have what is referred to as "selective deafness," that is, they only hear what they want to hear—like the squeak of a refrigerator door or the rustle of a candy bar wrapper.

Mac, a West Highland White Terrier, has perfected selective obedience. Mac is thirteen years old and totally deaf, so his owner, Karen, communicates with him through hand signals learned when he was in Utility. When he wants to stay outside longer, he simply turns his head so that he can't see the come signal.

Maybe we've given in and now allow an oldster to sleep on the bed and maybe we save the last bit of ice cream for our old friend, but that doesn't mean being allowed to bark uncontrollably or to mark territory in the house. She must take her medicine even if she doesn't want to. He must be restrained from biting the veterinarian even when he feels discomfort.

The same discipline that worked when the dog was young can be used now: a direct stare with a firm command. Older dogs should realize that you mean business from past experience. They know when

Conne Duea did teach an old dog new tricks. Scruffy learned this trick overnight.

Nine-year-old Chesapeake Goldie keeps out the chill with a knitted sweater. Goldie is often a third party on Danielle Kees's dates.

you raise your voice and say "NO!" that they'd better submit or else. It doesn't make any difference whether they remember what the "or else" is or not. It doesn't matter that you wouldn't really ban them to a tree in the backyard for the rest of their lives. All they know is that their lord and master has spoken.

Dogs are intelligent and can be taught amazing things—even when they've reached senior citizen status. They can learn that it's permissible to lie on "their" chair or the furniture with slipcovers, but never on the new couch. All it takes is some intensive training for a day or two with commands and follow-through.

Although it is possible to teach our dogs at any age, some things are stuck with glue and cannot be jarred loose. Dogs seem to have an internal time clock that sets off an alarm for important occasions. What else could explain a pet meeting the master at the back door every night at 6:00 P.M. or waiting at the front window for her friend to come home from school at 3:00 in the afternoon? This alarm also goes off at dinner, bed and walk times.

The canine's inborn timer, which is tuned to their people, can serve as a handy reminder. Unfortunately, it isn't always possible for us to meet their schedules, much as we'd like to.

Mary's Miniature Schnauzer, Lucy, knew that Mary came home from work at 11:00 P.M. Each night Lucy met Mary without fail. When Mary was called out of town for three months, she left Lucy at home. Mary's mother reported that at 11:00, Lucy sat by the window. She waited faithfully for an hour or two until she realized Mary wasn't coming home, then retired to the bedroom looking forlorn. Mary couldn't ask for a more dedicated friend.

Part of that instinct might be triggered by reading our body language and activities. The fun is in viewing their reaction to our actions.

Scruffy, Connie's eleven-year-old Wirehaired Fox Terrier, doesn't always interpret things correctly. "She associates housecleaning with the arrival of guests and patiently watches the front door. If we look out the window too often, she realizes we're expecting someone, perhaps a pizza delivery person, and she loves pizza crust. Since she never sees the entire pizza, she must think the box is filled with crusts!"

Scruffy also knows that if Connie wears shoes instead of slippers, she's going somewhere. But, most important, the little dog has learned that very small paper bags usually contain items bought at a pet store. Just like children, dogs anticipate gifts with delight.

April Fool's Carla CDX, TD, TDI, invites Linda Colflesh to play.

At age 11, Carla sometimes still enjoys a run at full speed.

When we can, we should keep things on an even keel, but sometimes, no matter how we try, their boat rocks in a storm. It's impossible to explain to a dog why we must occasionally disappoint them. All we can do is pay them back by loving them one tenth as much as they love us.

Hazel Dougall, 86, and her Chesapeake Cache, 15, on a beach outing. Cache waits for Hazel's daughter, Nancy Lowenthal, to throw the stick for a retrieve.

5

Shifting Gears

Precious
Seems the years flew by so fast,
  Can it be such time has passed?
Though haler years she may have seen,
I love her most at seventeen.
MELANIE GRIFFITH SPORER

CHANGE IS as much a part of life as shifts in the weather. We can't prevent some things from disrupting and interfering with our dogs' lives, but we can make it easier whenever a buzz threatens to interrupt the daily hum.

Many changes occur gradually or with advance warning, and just as we prepare ourselves for an eventuality, we can help our pets adapt. This is easily accomplished by reassuring them of our love and their status in our lives. No matter how many are added to the household, an old dog is always number one . . . or at least should be allowed to believe she is.

"The muzzle may be graying, the gait no longer bouncy, the hearing definitely not keen and the eyes sparkle through cloudiness, but with all this, Granny at thirteen years is still in charge," says her owner, Zona. Granny, known as Zestee in bygone days, rules the roost of four other Keeshonden.

Granny Zestee, waiting to be catered to by owner Zona Munro.

At age 16, "B.E." is willing to share his treat—even with a rabbit. Owner: Sue Bourcier.

Granny is still the top dog. "Occasionally Granny falls, but this does not thwart her dominance. No one dares approach her, as she picks herself up and immediately arches her neck and asserts herself.

"It is our turn now to cater to her. She has given us so much through the years and is still a bright spot every day for us. In some small way we hope to repay her for all the joy and devotion she has shared." So Granny Zestee shall remain top dog.

To make sure your grandma or grandpa stays at the top of the pack, simply allow yourself to enjoy all the wonderful things about your old dog. He no longer destroys anything by chewing, so constant vigilance isn't required.

Senior citizens are quite predictable and often sleep while you're away from the house. Hashimoto doesn't leave unwelcome surprises on the carpet; therefore he can have free run of the house. His greatest joy is to be by your side, and since he's well behaved, he can go with you on errands.

WHO'S IN CHARGE?

Many families enjoy having two or more dogs, who can take turns sharing privileges, such as house queen for the day or leading a parade to the mailbox on the corner. The older one often teaches doggie etiquette to the younger.

In multidog households, one usually becomes the pack leader. When that leader is lost, the pack mills about with no purpose until someone else climbs upon the throne and picks up the scepter. Kennel owners report that young males, or occasionally dominant females, may challenge one another much as animals do in the wild. Once the pecking order is worked out and everyone knows there's someone in charge again, life continues smoothly.

Katie's family of dogs always has a matriarch who rules the kingdom. Wirehaired Fox Terrier Muffy ruled until she was fifteen, when Trixie, a Pekingese mix, took over until she was thirteen. They were respected by the younger dogs and served as role models.

Trixie even helped train a new pup by pushing him toward the door and giving a disapproving woof whenever he goofed. When Trixie finished her meal and walked off, it was fair game for the younger set, but not until then. One day, as she lay close to her bowl, the others were unable to resist any longer and inched closer for the attack.

Trixie moved with the speed of a pup, pecking each one on the rear, reminding them of their manners. The bowl was hers until she turned her back on it.

Katie says that after Trixie's death, her other dogs did not know how to act without a ruler until her Shih Tzu, Ming, took over creating her own Ming dynasty until she was sixteen.

Self-imposed duties are also part of the teaching process.

Honey's job had always been mole patrol. The mini Dachshund took her job very seriously. When Toby entered her life, she taught him how to dig for moles. Never mind that Toby was a Corgi.

At fourteen, Honey was the senior member of the team and always made the kill. Toby respected that privilege. Their owner, Carol Ann, said that it was great fun seeing the two dogs work together, even if the Corgi was supposed to be herding, not hunting.

When two dogs have been close companions, the loss of one often leaves the other lonely and morose. They grieve when a pal dies, just as we do.

A new pup helps fill that empty spot and gives the older one something to do again. An empty-headed, bouncy baby requires an awful lot of training, which takes a tremendous amount of time, leaving absolutely none for moping. Genevieve wrote that a Keeshond pup brought her fifteen-year-old Poodle mix out of depression after the loss of the dog's ten-year-old pal.

Salty and Pepper, two Scottish Terriers, were sister and brother, always together ever since Lily had brought them home. They'd been great company for each other while Lily was at her job each day. Whenever Lily brought home a new toy, she brought two, a pink one for Salty and a blue one for Pepper.

When Pepper died at the age of nine, Salty lost her incentive to play and spent her days and nights lying on her blanket with a blue ball between her paws. Lily had to coax the Scottie to go for a walk. Lily says, "I know Salty missed Pepper and grieved for him. I'm sure she would have shed tears if that were possible. I actually thought I was going to lose her too because she lost weight, had chronic diarrhea and became listless.

Lily said about a week later they saw a black dog in the park. "For a minute, Salty perked up and her tail started wagging. Then he disappeared and she slowed down again, tail and head slumped. That afternoon I took her with me to visit a litter of Scottie pups, and Salty picked out ours."

Kahlua, a 12-year-old mix, is an old hand at Agility. She helps her seven-month-old friend, Spin, catch on to the teeter-totter. Owner: Judi Schott.

(L-R): CH Colacove Chimney Sweep, age 2, has good role models in CH Dasa's Red Rover CD, age 8, CH Colacove Brio Bacchanal CD, age 8, CH Colacove Night Dancer CDX, age 10, and Colacove Day Dreamer UDT, age 11. Owner: Karen Froemming.

Salty soon showed interest in eating and taking walks again. It wasn't long before Lily spied her playing with Cinnamon, trying to grab the pup's orange ball. She didn't begin romping and playing immediately, but she became alert and felt it was her duty to teach little Cinnamon how to behave.

"Four years later, she's still trying to teach him."

Other owners want to avoid the awful gap that occurs at the loss of a pet and decide to adopt a new dog while the first is still alive. If a second animal is added, it should be done, preferably, when the older one is in good health. Many times, the vivacity of youth sparks a bright flame in a life where there was only a dim flicker.

Suzanne insists that her ten-year-old Cocker could have been classified as old a year ago. But about that time, Pooh Bear entered his second puppyhood because of a new arrival named Spencer. It was as though Pooh had been waiting for Spencer all his life.

"All of a sudden, instead of sleeping all day, Pooh was wide awake, raring to go. There literally was a new sparkle in his eyes and a spring in his step. His new energy amazed us. He had always been on the lazy side. But not with Spencer! They play all the time, with each other and with toys we have had for years but which Pooh had always ignored. Pooh used to be spoon-fed but lately has started eating by himself. Pooh Bear has come out of a forced early retirement and is discovering his lost youth."

Adding puppies to a home where one dog has ruled supreme for many years is a ticklish situation. It might work out all roses as it did when Pooh accepted Spencer. Other times, adjustments must be made. Old dogs deserve to be treated as the patriarchs and matriarchs they are. They should be given priority over pups. Junior can learn to wait his turn; he'll have many years to be first after Pops is gone. When feeding, give the old man his bowl first. As they hunker down at your feet waiting for a nibble of popcorn, share with Gramps first, then his daughter and finally the littlest guy. There will be less jealousy, and if the alpha dog of the pack decides to assert his authority, the pup is likely to give in.

If the senior dog is territorial, introductions should be made on neutral ground. Away from home, there's no need for the oldster to strut about glowering, protecting both premises and rank. Acceptance comes easily because the stranger offers no threat. Once friendship seems imminent, a welcoming party can take place on the homefront with the old guy playing the part of the guest of honor and the youngster as an invited and suitably courteous guest.

Continue to supervise all play for a time. Owners should not make an assumption that all's well just because there's a tentative tail wag and sniff between the two. If the senior dog remains bossy, they should be separated when situations might prove testy: during mealtimes, when the owner is gone, when Pup becomes too pesty.

Despite the owner's preference to revere the aged, it becomes necessary for working dogs to pass the baton. They must do this smoothly and easily, allowing the usurper to take over. This can create jealousy when an animal has served most of its life not only as a pet but as a partner—a guide dog, for instance, or as a police dog. Occasionally the jealousy is serious enough that the older animal must be officially put out to pasture at the training headquarters or in another home. Other times the dog can be retired at home and accepts the role of pet. Some are mellow enough not to mind being the supporting actor rather than the star. A newspaper item told of a police officer who had dognapped her nine-year-old canine partner rather than allow him to be euthanized because of age. Good for her!

In some situations, following the older dog helps the newcomer learn the ropes.

Fred is a private investigator and owns a security company. He feels that young dogs watch and learn while participating in practice and real-life situations.

Fred's five-month-old German Shepherd, Brando, is already following in his father's pawsteps by accompanying the nine-year-old Cliff on his rounds with the detective. Brando's lessons range from simple to dangerous. The pup learned how to jump off the tailgate of the truck by hanging onto Cliff's tail.

On one patrol, a shot was fired. The older police dog alerted and began to search for the source. Young Brando observed and fearlessly attempted to follow.

Fred knew this was good training because Cliff was an example of a good student himself. Years before he had started his canine career by observing his predecessor, Paco, who had forty-five apprehensions over his nine years of service.

An animal who has become accustomed to being the boss or enjoying life as an "only dog" is more likely to accept another that recognizes his authority. This can be most easily achieved when the newcomer is a pup, a smaller breed or a dog of the opposite sex. Of course, one who is mild-mannered and submits to the dominant dog's will is unlikely to ruffle any furry feathers either.

Heineken, 13, and Robbie, 3, explore Heineken's new day-time insulated dog house. Owner: Susanne Maxwell.

Spatterdash Yawvin, age 14, and his daughter Mareg's Thea, age 12, lounging on their soft pillows. Owner: Margie Lachs.

Sometimes a dog appoints himself guardian.

We call this story "Fat Albert and His Fledglings." Fat Albert is a well-behaved Cocker/Beagle mix who always came when called. One night, however, he didn't. Owner Orville, heart in mouth, hurried out to see what was the matter. There on the ground was a baby bird. Orville went for a ladder and gently placed the fledgling back in the birdhouse. The family then put away the ladder and tried to coax the dog into the house. Still Albert refused to budge. They searched the surrounding area with a flashlight. Sure enough, there were two more babies. Once again the ladder was brought to the tree and the birds were put to bed. Three weeks later, Albert again played guardian when the houses needed to be moved. Even though his next-door nemesis, a German Shepherd with a large bark, raced along the fenceline, Albert lay beside the houses with stalwart heart until his charges were safe and secure in their homes.

BABIES ALL

When it comes to adding human babies to the existing family, it's a different story. In the ultimate scheme of things, people come first, and if the safety of a child is at stake, the dog must be the one to adjust or go.

This does not have to happen, however, if a family takes advantage of the nine-month waiting period and prepares the dog for changes.

Mikki was a bit spoiled, her owners admitted, and possessive of her toys. Obviously, this was going to take some work before their new baby arrived. To prepare Mikki, Dave and Laura began intensive pre-baby training. Laura explains, "We continued to show Mikki how much we loved her, but we did things a small child would do. I'd put her bowl down and after she'd had a few bites, take it away and add an extra goodie to her meal. Mikki thought that was great."

Laura laughed. "I could see her mind working: Someone takes away your bowl and you get more. So now and then I'd put in extra to begin with, then remove a little and give her a hug instead. So I guess she thought that wasn't so bad either."

Dave joined in. "We took her for walks and stopped to allow the neighborhood kids to pet her. I carried her ball and let the kids take turns throwing it for her. Eventually, we asked some children and their parents to our home. We were present to oversee all activity, although we were heart-in-mouth at the possibility of hair-pulling, using Mikki as a step stool to climb on the couch and the little girls teething on Mikki's ear."

Dave and Laura continued exposing Mikki to children, telling her how wonderful she was and giving the old dog lots of love. When they came home with their new baby, Mikki greeted them all with a wag.

If wise precautions are taken, dogs usually are good nannies. And if the Darlings' Nana in *Peter Pan* isn't part of their genetic makeup, at least they can learn to tolerate the young humans who have entered their lives.

A dog teaches a child compassion, responsibility and the realities of life, like aging and eventual loss. A child can experience totally unselfish love with no expectations. Given the chance, your dog can become your child's best friend. With proper socialization, training and preparation, rarely is there a need to "get rid of" the dog or banish your pet to the backyard.

Still, parents should supervise children and dogs, ready to discipline the offensive line and comfort the defensive one. Children shouldn't kick or pull the dog's hair, or use the dog as a step stool. Dogs shouldn't growl or knock over a child. Neither should bite. With *both trained* properly, kids and pets go together like peanut butter and jelly.

Even dogs who have been accustomed to being the "first child" can learn to accept an infant. Whether a dog is old or young, when a child moves into "his" house, it naturally moves the dog one rung farther down on the ladder.

A few animals who begrudge their position as low dog on the totem pole might buck and snort at this new overseer—a short, noisy one at that. When jealousy occurs, the dog should be given plenty of attention and exercise during the special time when your dog has your undivided attention, but your pet must be taught to understand that this little person is just one more boss in life.

Family growth and our mobile life-styles often mean bigger changes. Moving from one house to another can be a difficult adjustment for a canine senior. It's a busy time for people, packing, cleaning, fixing up, house hunting and taking care of all the necessary details. In all the hustle-bustle, few take the time to ponder the confusion the family pet may be feeling. Besides, the explanation can't be made in a language dogs understand.

If possible, the dog should be taken along to visit the new home

At 14, Hearing Dog Nugget looks forward to retirement and just playing with owner Larry
Burgess.   *N.E.A.D.S.*

before moving day. Play a quick game of fetch in the yard. Introduce your pet to the neighbors. Allow Bruno to sniff around the new house to his heart's content while you putter about.

If the move involves some distance, making a prior introduction impossible, make the change as calm as possible. Place the dog in a crate with a favorite toy and a soft towel or old flannel shirt bearing your scent. Reassure Bruno of your presence by taking him out for a walk now and then. Use a leash even if that's not your usual custom so that he doesn't take off in the middle of the hubbub or dart back into his familiar home just as the movers are carrying out your antique glassware. If he's accustomed to and accepts being boarded, you might want to consider boarding him for a day or two, again leaving toys and an item with the family's scent.

When the dog arrives at the new home, don't make the mistake one owner admitted. Dorothy discarded Fritz's old toys, bowls and blanket, buying new ones after the move. Her dog was confused and upset, broke training and moaned his complaints until Dorothy dug the ragged, beloved discards out of the trash.

Arrange all those old, comforting, good-smelling (to him!) toys and dishes in approximately the same area (for example, if he's always eaten in the kitchen along with you continue to feed him there at least for some time). Don't suddenly expect him to eat on the sun porch. If familiar things are there along with his favorite people, hey, this must be home!

Care must be taken that your elderly pet doesn't wander off, looking for more familiar surroundings. If you're going to be too busy to watch after her, confine her so that she'll be safe. As age takes its toll, and as swiftness, memories, hearing and/or vision fade, it is vital to watch our old folks carefully, even in well-known territory.

Jennifer's frightening story fortunately has a happy ending. "My Shetland Sheepdog, Shep, was fourteen years and three months when this adventure occurred. I live on twenty acres in Canada with two other dogs, both young. I walked them as usual in the late afternoon. Shep, who was totally deaf, would always tag along behind, off the leash, and arrive at the back door five minutes after me and bark to be let in. However, this day he had not returned after ten minutes, and I sensed something was wrong. I set off along our trails, quite expecting to find him dead."

Jennifer searched that day and the next, notified her neighbors and finally feared that a coyote must have found Shep. She says, "The days that followed were very difficult. Even though Shep always spent a great deal of time sleeping, at least I knew where he was and that he was content. Not to know how his life had ended, after we had shared so much, and not to have anything to bury or say good-bye to, was the hardest part."

Eleven days later she received a call that led to Shep. He was found fifteen miles away, eight days after his disappearance. Owner and dog were joyfully reunited.

Jennifer credits his survival to his condition and the fact that he was used to camping and hiking outdoors. "Christmas came in November for me that year! For the first couple of days after his return, he buried his face against my legs and just grunted in his throat—if ever a dog was trying to talk!"

Although she believes the misadventure has faded from his memory, she says it will never leave hers. "I learned two things: not to let him out of my sight when walking with him and to appreciate every day he's with me."

Clever owners continue to find ways to appreciate their dogs and to keep them young at heart. If you and the dogs have always shared breakfast, that's still possible. Just substitute a bowl of oatmeal or bran flakes for the gooey doughnut. When retrieves over a jump are no longer possible, fetching a stick from a shallow pond stimulates the mind as well as the body.

Jean found it hard to think of her Hungarian Kuvasz as old when she was asked to describe life with her thirteen-year-old for the Kuvasz Newsletter. She wrote that Dogga still loves to swim in the creek and play with stones. Jean weighed Dogga's most recent treasure, which the old dog carried proudly on a ten-minute uphill walk home from the creek, never once dropping the six-pound stone.

Dogga and Jean love to travel together, and they've been able to continue that pastime, thanks to a couple of concessions. Because Dogga's bladder is no longer dependable, Jean carries two large, cotton-lined, vinyl tablecloths, which she spreads on the floor—"like a wall-to-wall diaper." They're easily washable and make Dogga a welcome guest wherever the two go.

Arthritic joints may not be up to leaping over tall buildings, but they'll still take the dog around the block or around the yard. After Dogga made a few thwarted attempts at jumping into the car, Jean placed a step stool for Dogga's convenience. Now they can continue their travels.

Sandy MacGregor Von Hasselwick Am/Can CD, CG, age 13, is an accomplished actress. Owner: Hazel Wichman.

Something else has occurred over the years: Dogga's vocabulary has increased. This means that not only does Dogga understand the commands and words of love when Jean talks to her, but that her pet now recognizes the word "b-o-n-e" when it is spelled! Jean has considered speaking Hungarian, but then Dogga would probably become bilingual.

The wealth of knowledge our dogs learn and store over their lifetimes sometimes leads to a new career.

Not all changes are unwelcome or require rehearsal time. Some things can be altered overnight and be greeted with wags and enthusiasm.

Find additional ways to take advantage of your Utility training and the knowledge of hand signals. Karen rides horseback in parades with four of her obedience-trained Italian Greyhounds on long leads. They perform simple exercises, such as sits or downs in unison or consecutively, and are always a big hit.

NEW HORIZONS

Several old dogs have become actors. Well-behaved dogs who follow commands are in demand to fill parts on stage, for commercials and even in the movies. Carla, the Borzoi, joined actress Barbara Eden in selling furniture, lolling about on an "approved" piece and barking at a tacky one.

Sandy, a thirteen-year-old Border Terrier, is a local celebrity. She played Toto in school productions of The Wiz *and Sandy in* Annie, *receiving a standing ovation as her namesake in the latter play. Following this, owner Hazel says she was contacted by an animal talent agency in New York looking for a dog who would retrieve a sneaker. Hazel told the agency she'd call them back, went out and threw a sneaker for Sandy. She called the agency and said, "No problem." So Sandy was signed on to play an abandoned dog in the motion picture* Running on Empty. *Sandy is far from a stray, but she was a pro, following hand signals and verbal commands.*

Many people turn to volunteer work as they find more time on their hands. When the days are no longer filled with a family's demands or the restrictions of employment, we can use the time to help others. Dog owners find that one pleasurable way to fill their old dogs' spare time is through demonstrations or simply love-ins for people whose days are otherwise very much the same.

Louise makes regular visits to nursing homes with her English Cockers. When Louise feels a dog is too old to jump, she has it do the spelling trick. She brings along several large white wooden letters and scrambles them up on the floor. The dog makes five trips to the jumbled letters, picks one out and brings it to Louise, who places it on a red board. Of course, it's all done by scent discrimination, but the surprise and delight of the patients who think the dog is spelling "Hello" make their visit a hit. And the canine senior eats up the applause.

Following the show, each dog makes the rounds. Louise points out the age of her oldest dogs: "This dog is fourteen, and that's over a hundred in 'people age.'"

Nursing homes and some hospitals and other institutions welcome the entertainment offered by obedience demonstrations and therapeutic dog visits. Several organizations have developed programs and certify dogs as official therapy workers. The dogs often wear brightly colored hats or sweaters or a jaunty bandana for their excursions, and an aura of excitement is in the air for canines and humans alike.

Cary was proclaimed therapy dog of 1989 by the Delta Society. Cary, a Golden Retriever, was instrumental in a Michigan program that involves more than sixty dogs and their owners who regularly visit at least a dozen nursing homes. Betty Jean, a veterinarian, had envisioned the concept and gave a presentation at one nursing home in 1978. It met with underwhelming enthusiasm "until, after a release from me, Cary started around the room. She went from one person to another, quietly wagging her tail, laying a head in a lap or nudging a hand for petting. She always made you feel that she loved you. Cary sold the plan."

The Golden went on to be an ambassador for the program, appearing on television, in the newspaper and in a video. Recently, Cary developed lymph node cancer and has been on chemotherapy. Betty Jean tried to leave her at home, but the dog was unhappy, so she continues to attend the sessions, visiting for as long as she wants. This dog, and others like her, cheer days that are dreary for humans who suffer too.

Oldsters have a special feeling for one another. Visiting an institution as therapy dogs or strutting their stuff in a demonstration at a nursing home brightens the day for all.

Several of the patients have owned pets and miss them. They welcome an unobtrusive visitor, one who doesn't pry or scold or shift from foot to foot, anxious to leave, one who only sits by their side in perfect contentment.

Louise Shattuck's English Cockers, CH Carry-On Catch A Minnow UDT, age 12; Coltrim Cream Tea CDX, TD, age 14; and CH Carry-on Rackety Coon CDX, TD, age 14, spell out a greeting at a nursing home visit.

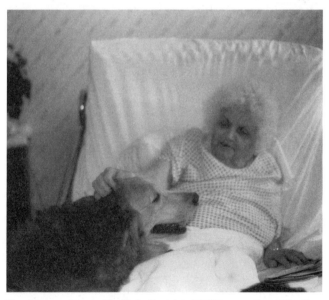

Cary UD, age 12, was The Delta Society's 1989 Therapy Dog of the Year. Owner: Betty Jean Harper, DVM.

Tammara of Twisted Oaks CDX, U-CDX, age 10, pulls her covered wagon in parades. Owner: Betty Luttier.

Michael Duke of Magnus, age 10, was active beyond the average lifespan of large dogs, such as Great Danes. Owner: Paddy Magnuson.

Debbie says her dogs often accompany her to work as a case manager for the mentally ill and that her patients welcome the animals. Debbie adopted one of the dogs, Max, after he had a tussle with a brown bear in her driveway.

Road construction in the mountains had driven the bears toward the community. Max, who lived in the neighborhood, had always roamed, but he reached the end of his nonexistent rope when he ran into the bear.

Debbie's dogs gave the alarm at 4:00 A.M. Halloween night, and she rose to hear the growls and whines of a terrific battle. After the fury died down, Debbie notified the sheriff's department and began to search for the dog.

She says, "I found him lying in his own yard, weak and in distress. His owner expressed no interest in providing assistance." Debbie drove Max to a vet, who diagnosed multiple fractures of a leg and a cut artery.

Three days later, Max came home to a new and caring owner—Debbie. She says, "Working with mentally ill people has shown me that dogs take you for who you are regardless of what's wrong with you. I don't work with a single client that my dogs don't adore. Maybe dogs could teach us people a thing or two."

Two Cairn Terriers, Pojo (sixteen) and Tammie (a mere ten-plus), visit nursing homes as a part of Project Pup. Pojo has cataracts and is nearly blind. Betty says that she still occasionally takes him to some of the smaller homes where she can carry him most of the time. "The old folks really identify with him."

The younger Tammie entertains the groups by pulling a child's wagon, sometimes disguised as a "surrey with the fringe on top" or a covered wagon. She loves doing it so much that she helps move some of the light-weight equipment in her wagon for a demonstration. Tammie has her AKC CDX, just completed her UKC (United Kennel Club) U-CDX and participates in Agility competition.

Dreamer, an Italian Greyhound, prefers to visit the homes after lunch. His owner, Karen, says that many of the residents have crumbs on their sweaters or in mustaches which Dreamer proceeds to clean off. He also sits in on a game of cards if there's an empty chair, and that's "always good for a laugh."

The Delta Society is an organization that promotes animal/human

Colacove Day Dreamer UDT, Whippet, at age 11, charms the residents in a local nursing home. Owner: Karen Froemming.

Roy, an 11-year-old Border Collie, has represented Scotland at the International Sheepdog Trials for the past nine years. He's been Scottish National Champion three times. Owner John Templeton, of Ayrshire, Scotland, says he is fit enough to compete again this year.

bonding. Their 1989 survey showed that half of the physicians, psychiatrists and physiologists polled recommended pet therapy, especially for loneliness and depression.

Studies have shown that people with pets live longer and are mentally and physically healthier. Geriatric therapists say a pet helps fill the gap left when people live alone. A dog gives them someone to talk to, someone to caress and someone who needs *them*. Studies have shown that the survival rate after hospitalization and coronary disease is higher among pet owners. It has also been proved that blood pressure lowers when stroking a pet.

All of these studies encouraged former President Reagan and Congress to pass the 1983 Federal Fair Housing Act, which gives elderly or handicapped tenants the right to keep pets in federally funded housing.

The joy and camaraderie of institutionalized people is obvious when dogs visit—no studies necessary. Animals have been known to calm the mentally disturbed, awaken long dormant interest in Alzheimer patients and promote tranquility even in prisons.

Therapeutic visits and demonstrations have become accepted and welcomed in nursing homes and even some hospitals. Various groups have organized throughout North America to offer therapy dog certification.

Older adult dogs are gentle and trustworthy with patients. Puppies, being puppies, might be too rambunctious and seldom content to stay in one place for long.

Utilizing these old dogs to cheer others serves as therapy for everyone. Patients wait for the visiting day eagerly, the dogs have a spring in their step at being spruced up and going somewhere, and owners renew the bond once so close during the active days when all were younger. Dogs who are no longer able to leap over jumps or circle the rings are able to compete with anyone when it comes to warming hearts and brightening otherwise tedious days.

CH Crafdal Thor Mhors Paulette UDT, age 10, was the first Champion Norwegian Elkhound to earn a UDT. Owner: Paul and Nina Ross.

6

The Reclining Years

My legs will no longer take me for a run,
Still my desire is strong like when I was young,
    My eyes no longer see clear,
My master's voice I do not always hear.
    So I escape into my sleep,
Where my days afield I keep,
    And I can be young again,
Running the fields with my friends.

J. SYNSTAD

As OUR DOG'S HAIR turns to silver and we realize the golden years are here and now, we wish we could add days to those years. Humans are constantly reminded by the media to "watch cholesterol . . . check your blood pressure . . . eat bran . . . exercise regularly." And we think maybe what's good for us is good for our dogs. We *can* do a great deal, as owners, to help our dogs live a long, high-quality life.

Some dogs are born chow hounds and their only exercise is walking to the food bowl. If our dog eats everything that doesn't run fast enough, it's up to us to adjust her diet and lengthen the walk.

Diet and exercise are important parts of maintaining good health. People know that prevention of disease helps ensure a long and healthy life. We're cutting down on fat and salt, exercising more and watching our stress levels. It's no different with our dogs—except they can't do it for themselves. We've got to do it for them.

Preserving health is an important factor in enjoying our dogs for a long time and, in turn, for our dogs to enjoy a quality life. Of course, there are no guarantees in life, and a young marathoner might have a heart attack, or the meticulously cared for dog could still develop cancer. The best we can do is increase the odds by following the formula for disease prevention and good health.

Scientists have chronicled and confirmed the factors that lengthen life span. The acronym "LONGEVITY" incorporates these factors to remind us how to help our dogs achieve that goal.

Lifetime care
Observation
Nutrition
Genetics
Environment: Stress-free
Veterinary Care
Industry
TLC
You

LIFETIME CARE

The seeds we sow during our dog's puppyhood are reaped as rich rewards in later life. From the moment we acquire our dog, at six weeks or six years, a good routine of proper care lengthens the road toward old age. This is one time we don't want to take any shortcuts because the condition of a geriatric pet reflects the care and treatment received during its lifetime.

Enroll your dog in the Head Start program. Routine veterinary care, including annual vaccinations, parasite exams and health checks, are the first habit to establish. Over time, establish an on-going health record at your chosen veterinary clinic and develop a working relationship with the veterinarian and his or her staff. A good rapport helps immensely when medical treatment becomes necessary.

Linda's ten-year-old Rottweiler, Jak, has cysts all over, ranging in size from a walnut to a tennis ball. Linda was relieved when the vet

CH Windhaven's Peregrination CD, JH, age 11, retrieving her 67th (yes, that's correct!) bird of the day. Owner: Judy Ford.

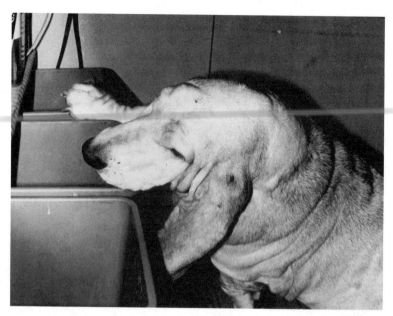

CH Bernmar's Theodor-Edward Bear, age 13, attempts to supplement his diet by snitching from the food bins. Owner Peggy Bommersbach caught him in the act.

Maggie loves every minute of her weekly hands-on massage. Owner: Barb Turek.
Kathy Cragg

assured her they were not cancerous, and she has not bothered to have them removed.

Recently, however, when Jak tried to turn too fast, he put pressure on a brittle bone, tore ligaments in his leg and broke the bone. Even though the surgery was expensive, Linda said, "my vet knows me very well; there was never any discussion about putting him to sleep due to his old age."

She says he is recovering well and that Jak is still very alert, protective and, most of all, loving.

Older animals are also more susceptible to extremes in weather. Dehydration or heat exhaustion is more common, which makes housing and protection from the elements more than luxury. They are a necessity. Dampness and drafts cause pain and stiffness. Don't allow an older dog to lie in front of an air conditioner or heating duct. One chills and the other dries skin and can even burn a dog whose senses are not as keen.

Moving an outdoor dog in at night is advisable, such as Susanne did with Heineken when he turned sixteen. Although the Husky mix thrived in cold weather and always adjusted his activities to his internal thermostat, Heineken is now relishing the luxury of being indoors with the family.

Most dogs accept gradual change. If we are aware of a slowing down, we can prepare our buddies for a life in the recliner instead of on the treadmill.

Fortunately, dogs don't have many bad habits that need to be changed. Dogs don't crave cholesterol or caffeine. They don't smoke or do drugs. Their favorite spot is by your side, not at the corner tap or behind the wheel of a fast car. Neuter them and they'll never look longingly at anyone but you. So, as they enter their golden years, they don't need to curtail all their activities.

A lifetime routine of training, exercise, grooming, proper housing, dental care and good nutrition contributes to a golden old age. Basic training of some sort helps the dog accept handling and restraint, a necessity in case of illness requiring hospitalization or extensive home care. It also teaches your dog to focus on you, an aid when hearing or vision begins to diminish. Besides, training—like grooming—is time spent together, good for its own sake as well as to provide the opportunity to notice changes when they first occur.

Three generations of healthy Beardies, CH Arcadia's Virginia Slim ROM, age 4, CH Arcadia's Midnight Munday ROM, age 7, and "grandma" CH Rich-Lin's Molly of Arcadia ROMX, age 9. Owners: Diann Shannon and Judi Pruitt.

Bearded Collie CH Arcadia Peppermint Schnapps ROM, age 9, reflects the good care she has received throughout her life. Owners: Diann Shannon and Tori Simpson.

OBSERVATION

You, the owner, can truly be your old dog's best friend just by closely observing Spot on a regular basis. Use your senses—sight, sound, touch and smell—all sharpened by love. Any changes can be noticed immediately and evaluated before they progress to something more serious.

Look at your dog with an analyst's eye. Taking a moment to watch your senior's morning routine is like reading a diary. Is it taking Spot longer to negotiate the stairs to the backyard? Begin to look for other signs of stiff joints or muscle pain. Do his bones appear more prominent? Perhaps he has lost weight or his muscles are wasting. Does he hesitate before going out at dusk? Maybe those aging eyes aren't seeing as well in dim light. Watch for any changes in gait, attitude or alertness. When you first think you notice something, jot it down on a calendar. Then you can make periodic comparisons and note progression or remission.

Tawny, an eleven-year-old German Shepherd, often played in the yard with her pal Ninja. She seemed to be fine and then, without warning, her hind legs tangled and she fell. Bill worried that the young male was too rough. But at Tawny's monthly bath and grooming session, her owners noticed that her rear nails were worn down, as though she had been dragging her rear feet.

At the next routine visit, Bill mentioned the symptoms to the vet, who suggested scheduling diagnostic work. After a complete physical, blood tests and radiographs of the hips and spine, Tawny was pronounced healthy except for a severe case of spinal arthritis.

Her exercise now consists of slow on-leash walks on level surfaces, and she takes pain relievers when she has bad days. At nearly thirteen, Tawny is enjoying a happy but more sedate life, content to watch through the window at Ninja roughhousing with the neighbor's Collie.

Marking changes in your dog's play, sleep, eating and bathroom habits can give you the first indication of a change in health. Be aware not only of the amount of food your pet is eating, but how fast the dog eats it or whether there is difficulty swallowing. Note particularly the amount of water consumed. An increase in water intake may signify internal disease. Watch bowel and urine elimination to record any change or abnormality.

Our eyes aren't the only senses that can note changes—listen.

Brandy, age 11, can still keep up with owner Marie Smiley on their daily runs.

Markay's Carolina Smoke CD, a 12-year-old Smooth Collie, despite blindness and arthritis, still enjoys a day at the beach. Owner: Eileen Parsons.

Does your dog pant when coming up the basement steps? Do you notice snoring, coughing or snorting that wasn't present previously? Does the dog's stomach sound like your grandmother's old wringer washer, gurgling and sloshing? Make notes of these things and ask your vet about them if they persist. You should also listen when your dog communicates to you with more subtle sounds. A murmur of pain, a whimper of discomfort or a sigh of apathy should be taken seriously.

Common Senses: Warning Signs by Sound, Smell, Touch and Sight

Sound

At first, Al thought he was imagining things, but Lucky's bark seemed to be higher pitched. He felt a bit sheepish mentioning it to the veterinarian when he brought the eight-year-old Dandy Dinmont in for his annual heartworm test and geriatric exam. Al made a joke about how when a boy's voice changed it became lower, not higher. But upon examination, the vet discovered a laryngeal polyp. This was successfully and simply removed, and Lucky once again became a baritone instead of a soprano.

Smell

If you smell something unusual, try to determine the source. Abnormal body discharges, especially those associated with infection, have strong, unpleasant odors. If your pal has bad breath, lift her lips and examine the teeth and gums. Ear odor, likewise, should prompt a careful look into the ear canal. Stronger than normal urine smell, a sudden increase in gassiness and a malodorous vaginal discharge are all red flags, signaling you to head to the vet.

Touch

The most important routine observation of your dog can be accomplished by something pleasurable to both of you—touch. Simply an extension of petting and grooming, massage allows you to emphasize awareness of the oldster. Since you probably spend lots of time stroking that graying head anyway, expand it into a "whole body massage." Your dog will love it, and you'll find any abnormalities early on.

As you gently work your way over every square inch of your dog's anatomy, be alert for changes. Fatty cysts are common in old-sters, but any lump should be checked out by a veterinarian.

The most obvious changes are lumps, sores or bumps not only in the skin but also in the joints, muscles, abdomen and so on. Be especially aware of breast masses in females. Make a note of any thickening or bump and mark it down, comparing it to a common object. If the pea-sized lump you notice in April becomes the size of a marble in May and like a walnut on the fourth of July, your vet will probably advise removal and a biopsy.

An astute owner is also aware of the tone and firmness of muscles, noting atrophy (shriveling or wasting). Changes in the texture or thickness of the hair coat (usually thinner or drier), color of the skin or mouth tissues and the flexibility of the joints can all indicate a problem. Drainage or discharge from anywhere is a warning alarm. Pain or discomfort can also be noted during your hands-on session.

Sight

Animals aren't capable of hypochondria or looking for sympathy. Actually, older dogs are often stoic and even great discomfort or advanced disease may be borne with quiet acceptance. Dogs who don't feel well might appear to turn inward, shutting out the world as they deal with the inner pain. Thus, a dog who no longer seems to care, doesn't get up to greet you or has lost interest in daily life shouldn't be shrugged off as merely aging.

Overt signs such as a bloated belly, emaciation or severe cough can come months or even years after little, initial symptoms begin. If the dog is tied out in the yard or banished to the garage without any routine daily care, signs may be missed until it is too late. And all that time suffering continued, even if borne in silence.

But if we are in tune with our dogs, if we truly observe them through eyes of love, we can notice subtle changes. We can be on top of medical problems before they become unbearable and/or untreatable.

NUTRITION

Proper nutrition is of paramount importance in prolonging the active, healthy years of an aging dog. The field of canine nutrition is

At age 12, Benji's alert look is testimony to owner's Mary & Jerry Beverase's watchful eyes and good care.

just now coming of age, and scientists are finding that proper nutrition may moderate the process of senility and aging.

The single most important nutritional factor in the aging dog is controlling weight. It's not easy. Over and over, our correspondents wrote, "Her favorite thing is eating." How do you deny a beloved friend who has so few enjoyments left? It's not easy to find substitutes for those tummy-warming breakfasts, yummy coffee breaks, gourmet feasts and midnight snacks. But it's necessary. Try substituting a walk or a head rub or a carrot for most of the above, and it will do both owner and dog a world of good.

Break the occasional treat in half; a small piece is as good as a big one. Try a low-fat, high-fiber dog biscuit for a snack that's healthy. Antacids help a gurgling or upset stomach, and rice can be substituted for a meal if stools become loose. Supplement a skimpy dinner with low-cal cooked veggies such as green beans or pumpkin. *Stay away from canned vegetables that have salt added.*

As with humans, obesity is a common denominator in many serious disorders. The increased work load of sending blood through the clogging fat and removing waste from all the extra poundage puts unnecessary stress on an aging heart and tired kidneys. Fat surrounds and displaces organs, further weakening diminished muscles. The gradual decrease in activity and metabolic requirements results in as much as a 20 percent decrease in energy needs for an aging dog. Therefore, continuing the diet of his robust youth is merely an invitation to unhealthy fat accumulation.

Diets created for older, less active dogs have a lower caloric density for assisting in weight control. This is usually achieved through additional fiber and moderation in fat, protein, phosphorus and sodium, a much healthier way to maintain weight than simply feeding less food. Grossly obese dogs may require specialized reducing diets prescribed by a veterinarian. Dog food for "less active dogs," hence many seniors, is found in many grocery stores and through the feeding programs of most large dog food companies.

Princess, a ten-year-old Pug, had bad breath and was in desperate need of a thorough dental cleaning. Due to her overweight condition, however, the veterinarian hesitated putting her under anesthesia. Her owner said she panted constantly, resisted going for walks and showed no interest in playing. He put Princess on "light" kibble and began walking her a half mile each morning and night. Now, ten pounds lighter and teeth sparkling, Princess looks forward to her walks. Larry said, "I thought I was being kind in sharing my nightly ice cream with her. Now she gets a chewbone to help keep her waistline, and it's better for her teeth too."

Beyond the Bulge: Internal Organs

Other important dietary considerations exist even in aging dogs that have maintained their youthful figures. As dogs age, gradual loss of the functional tubule components of the kidney is common, whether they're big, strong carting dogs or tiny, spoiled lapdogs. The major waste product of the kidney is urea, formed from the breakdown of excess proteins. As fewer and fewer kidney tubules are working to rid the body of the same amount of waste, the added workload aids and abets the further destruction of the remaining tubules.

A multitude of other internal organ functions are affected by even the most minute changes in the kidney's efficiency. Increased blood pressure creates a burden on the heart, slowly leading to congestive heart failure. The less efficient heart decreases blood flow through the kidneys, forcing a heavier work load on the already compromised organ.

The kidneys normally produce a factor that stimulates the production of new blood cells in the liver and bone marrow. Chronic kidney patients tend to be anemic, and the progressive reduction in oxygen-carrying capacity leads to further stress on the heat and, thus, to the kidneys. Inefficient kidney tubules create an increase in blood phosphates and, subsequently, a decrease in blood calcium. This leads to a leaching out of calcium from the bones. The imbalance of minerals in the serum allows the blood to become too acid, which contributes to many chronic problems, including further loss of bone calcium. The kidney is responsible for metabolizing vitamin D into a usable form, necessary for the absorption of calcium from the intestine. Therefore less calcium is taken from the diet and even more is removed from the bones. Many other complicated processes exist, but the pattern is obvious. They all create the well-known vicious circle that feeds on itself, spiraling downward toward kidney failure and death.

Although the kidney's aging process is to some extent inevitable, the cycle can be slowed considerably by a change in diet. The important factor here is a lower protein diet. When only enough protein to take care of the body's immediate needs is provided, there is less excess to be broken down into urea and excreted by the kidney.

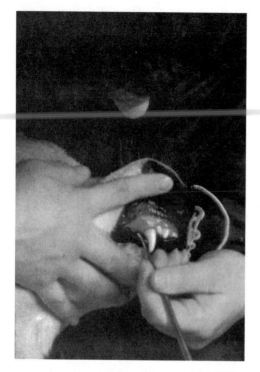

Good dental care, including scaling your dog's teeth, can prolong your pet's healthy life. Owner: Renée Stockdale.

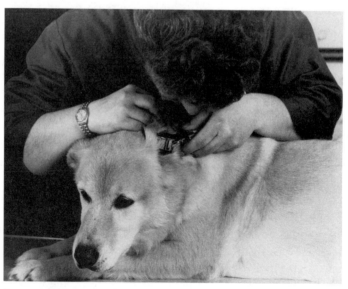

An occasional ear examination can identify problems before they become serious.

Frequent nail trims helps an old dog keep good footing. Models: Buck and Patty Tuck. Owner/credit: Renée Stockdale.

Patty draws blood from Buck for an annual heartworm test and chemistry panel. Owner: Renée Stockdale.

The level of sodium chloride (salt) also should be lowered in diets for dogs with impaired kidney function, and the balance of calcium and phosphorus needs to be adjusted. Of course, in restricted diets, the exact formulation of the ingredients is critical. The fact that low-protein diets slow the progress of existing kidney disease is well known; there is now some evidence that these restricted diets, begun in middle age, may actually forestall some of the initial tubule damage. In other words, they may be preventive as well as therapeutic.

Decreased sodium is also important for other age-related problems, such as heart disease. Amelioration of diabetes, pancreatic and digestive inefficiency, as well as chronic constipation, is aided by a higher fiber content, as is weight control.

Meeting Nutritional Needs

Almost all dog food companies have heeded the results of current nutritional research and now produce diets specifically formulated for older and/or less active dogs. These preventive diets are lower in salt and protein (only around 14 to 16 percent of high-quality protein instead of the 25 percent or greater formulations of most adult dog foods), have a proper calcium/phosphorus balance for the aging kidney and have a moderately higher fiber content.

Prescription diets that are specially formulated to assist in the treatment of specific disorders are also available. These will be discussed further in the next chapter.

Discuss dietary choices for your middle-aged or senior canine with your dog's veterinarian. Ask when they should be initiated. Eliminate any high-salt food or treats (especially the semimoist "burger" type dog foods) Avoid high-protein diets, or those that indicate protein levels appropriate for "active adults." Stay away from cheap or generic dog foods, since the quality of ingredients becomes increasingly critical as the amounts are reduced.

Check dog food labels and beware of anything containing "by-products." This could mean poultry beaks, feet, even feathers. Foods containing 14 percent poorly digestible protein (one of low biological value) could actually lead to malnutrition. A good quality food specially formulated for the aging pet is well worth the few pennies more and is less costly than attempting to correct a problem already on its way.

GENETICS

Once your dog is approaching old age, the genetic influence is a fait accompli. In fact, once you have chosen your companion—even as an eight-week-old pup—everything he has or ever will have genetically is already bundled up inside that squirmy, cuddly little body—even how quickly he'll gray! Because genetics strongly influences health, it is necessary to consider its effect when breeding or selecting a dog.

Laying the groundwork for health and longevity starts before your dog is born. Hundreds of factors concerning health are inherited; therefore, general life span has a basis in heredity. If your heart is won by a mixed breed from the pound, so be it. But, as in all cases of love at first sight, you must be willing to take your chances because there is no way of being sure what has gone into your dog's makeup.

Perry is truly a grande dame—a Champion, CD, JH (Junior Hunter), TT (Temperament Tested). Judy chose her German Wirehaired Pointer wisely. The structure that earned Perry her Championship also helped her toward her other titles and, most important, to reach her thirteenth birthday still in good health. Her JH title came at the age of eleven, won in four straight tries, with three perfect "10" scores. As Judy says, not bad for a great-grandmother.

With purebred stock, buyers can be selective. They can take the time to consider and to buy from knowledgeable breeders who have studied about and selected from sound, healthy individuals. Dogs with a congenital tendency to hip dysplasia, spondylosis (spinal arthritis) or other degenerative bone diseases, for example, are less likely to enjoy life and will suffer more. Their life span is often shorter because of chronic pain and weakness. A familial tendency to cancer, heart disease or kidney or liver failure certainly lessens the quality of life in later years. Small dogs, in general, live longer than large dogs, with all other factors being equal. But a genetically sound big guy can outlive a poorly bred peanut.

Mary chose her lines well when she began breeding Soft-Coated Wheaten Terriers. Her well-known show dog, a sire of numerous champions, is thirteen years old, in robust health and still standing at stud. His mother lived to fifteen-plus, as did his grandmother. If he were less genetically sound, he might have been seeing vets long before the age of thirteen instead of visiting ladies.

CH Acadian Boris of Kirtland, shown here at a Mastiff Specialty at age 8, lived to 14, well past the average age for his breed. Owner: William Harris.

Am/Can/Bda CH Bihar's Revenge of Sammi Raja winning Best of Breed at the Lhasa Apso National Specialty at the age of 11. "Tux" won the ALAC Veterans class every year from 1985–1989. Owner: Carol Strong.

ENVIRONMENT: STRESS-FREE

Inevitably, changes occur in our tissues and organs as we age, and it is no different for canines. There is no magic night cream to wipe away their wrinkles. The skin becomes thinner and less elastic; the liver, pancreas and stomach produce fewer digestive enzymes; and the lungs lose some of their efficiency and ability to ward off disease.

As discussed in the section on nutrition, kidneys lose a portion of their functional tissue. Hormonal glands become less productive, and there is a progressive loss of muscle and bone mass, along with a gradual decrease in cardiac output. Blood cell replacement lags, and there is a marked drop in immunocompetence. The transmission of messages through the nerves slows, and a gradual loss of vision and hearing occurs.

While most of these changes may not be immediately apparent on observation, they are happening and all have one thing in common. They may not affect the dog's ability to live a high-quality life under the best of conditions, but they definitely reduce the capability to respond to and deal with stress. For example, a less efficient digestive system may continue working well when the dog is fed a high-quality food, while a cheap, poor-quality product may cause emaciation in the same animal.

It's up to us to control our dogs' environment as they age, providing maximum comfort with minimum stress. We have to be careful to keep some things the same in order to lower stress, while other factors have to be altered or adjusted.

Housing, too, becomes a more critical issue than it is in youth. An old fellow may maintain weight and good attitude if kept inside, yet go into immediate decline if kenneled outdoors. Thinning skin requires more heat. Yet, at the same time, the reduction in muscle mass and slowed nerve conduction make the continual shivering that helps maintain body warmth much more difficult. Even if kenneled outside in the summer, oldsters may have to be brought in during the inclement days.

In nursing homes, many of the elderly patients wear sweaters or have a shawl over their shoulders even during warm weather. Most don't like air conditioning or drafts and prefer to bask in the sun.

We who run canine nursing homes should take the same care to avoid chilling our ancient friends. Warm, soft blankets or rugs comfort old bones. It may be advisable to order sweaters, coats and even boots for short-haired dogs or those with longer coats thinned by advancing years.

Cleaning Up

The immune system no longer works to full capacity and makes the senior more susceptible to infection. We can minimize the chances for contagion and disease in several ways. Yearly boosters must be continued for protection. As dogs become too stiff to clean themselves or to wear off dirt through exercise, it becomes more important to brush and bathe them whenever they are soiled. Coupled with good nutrition, cleanliness helps bolster the defenses.

Nevertheless, the worst source of germs can thrive within your dog—in an infected mouth. Oral hygiene and continuous dental care are more than niceties, they are keys to a healthy old age. Rotten, infected teeth are more insidious than simply offensive. Infection spreads to the gums, tonsils and lymph nodes, causing painful swallowing, vomiting from chronic drainage and sometimes fever. These germs can even journey through the bloodstream to other parts of the body including the heart valves, kidneys, liver, joints and elsewhere to set up satellite infections.

Anna thought her car knew the way to the veterinary clinic by itself. She'd made so many trips for Schnapps, who'd been vomiting, had chronic tonsillitis and just wasn't feeling herself. Anna hadn't wanted to have the eight-year-old Schnauzer's teeth removed because she thought it would make Schnapps look awful. But after six months of treatment, and lab work showing that all else was normal, she gave in. Schnapps had seventeen rotten teeth that were removed, and the rest were cleaned. Two years later, Schnapps is acting like a pup. Now Anna brushes Schnapps's teeth as part of her weekly grooming. She adds, "I should have had this done sooner—it's more important that Schnapps feel well than have a full mouth of teeth."

Talk to your veterinarian about the status of your dog's teeth and gums and schedule a dental appointment if recommended. After your old friend's choppers gleam again, you can keep them that way by frequent brushing or scaling at home. Your veterinarian or her technician can demonstrate the correct technique. The dog's fresh breath and healthy mouth are worth the effort. Loose, cracked or decayed teeth should be repaired or removed. Although there are no false teeth for dogs, they don't munch corn on the cob anyway and can eat amazingly well without some teeth.

VETERINARY CARE

Next to you, the veterinarian and veterinary medical resources are your dog's best chance for a healthy life. The modern veterinarian wants to be more than a firefighter who works to put out blazing diseases and infections, coming to the rescue after a crisis. She prefers to be a working partner helping you maintain the health of your dog.

Owners tend to think of neutering as a method of birth control and behavior modification, yet surgical alteration is a major choice to assist in assuring our pets a healthy old age. Early spaying prevents uterine and ovarian cancers, dangerous infections of the uterus, false pregnancies, mastitis and the majority of breast cancers. Castration eliminates testicular cancers and orchitis, as well as infection, and averts chronic enlargement and many cancers of the prostate. Even dogs that are a part of a planned breed program can be neutered following retirement or at a particular age.

Sally was a valuable brood bitch that had produced many champions and had built a solid foundation for Diann's kennel. But when the Beardie turned seven, it was time for Diann to move on and to take advantage of what Sally had produced. Sally was spayed, became the kennel matriarch and is spending the rest of her years playing with the grandpups and great-grandpups. And, with luck, at age thirteen, she might make it to the great-great-greats.

Depending on the breed's prime time, geriatric checkups should become a yearly ritual, along with the heartworm test and annual inoculations. Heartworms and disease are particularly disastrous to old dogs. Scientists tell us that the single most important factor that has increased the average life span of our dogs is the control of infectious diseases by vaccination.

Because of the less efficient immune system, however, fewer antibodies are produced and these don't last as long. The vaccine stimulates the body to produce antibodies that protect it from invading germs. Annual boosters stimulate the production of more immune factors before the levels drop low enough to allow disease to take hold.

Vaccinations to fight canine distemper virus and canine parvovi-

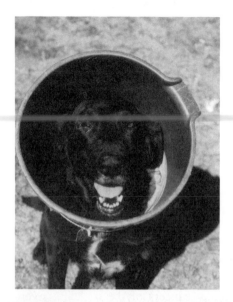

Trekker, 12-year-old Lab mix, tolerates a homemade Elizabethan collar which prevents scratching at stitches for a tumor removal. Owner: Lin Kozlowski.

Am/Can CH Five Oaks Pistol Pete, OFA Excellent, winning Best of Breed at nearly eleven years old. He and his get won twenty-two Specialty stud dog classes showing that good genes and good veterinary care go hand in hand. Owners: Richard and Ingrid Fox.

rus are vital. Depending on your veterinarian's advice and the area in which you live, shots may also include hepatitis (adenovirus II), parainfluenza, coronavirus, Leptospirosis and Bordatella. Rabies, too, should be kept up to date even if your dog has no chance of being exposed to a rabid animal. If Bruno should scratch or bite someone—whether or not it's accidental—most state laws force impounding an unvaccinated dog. This stress and expense can be easily avoided by keeping the rabies vaccination current.

When making the appointment for shots and heartworm test, tell the receptionist you'd appreciate a few minutes extra to talk to the doctor about any problems you've noted. Many veterinarians recommend special workups for their geriatric patients, to include a thorough physical examination (eyes, ears, skin, joints, throat, heart, abdomen and reproductive organs) as well as a complete blood count (CBC) and routine chemistry panel. Depending on the results, the rest of the examination can be tailored to the particular dog and her specific problems.

Radiographs, an electrocardiogram, ultrasound tests or further specific blood tests may also be advised. Armed with the conclusions, your veterinarian can discuss diet, medications, necessary procedures, changes in management and/or other considerations that will help your old gal maintain her health.

The chemistry profile is a wonderful screening tool that indicates early kidney, liver, heart, hormonal, infectious or other internal deficits while they can still be managed with medication and diet. Most of these panels test for fifteen to twenty substituents (enzymes, salts, minerals, proteins and others) for a nominal fee (generally less than $30) and a small amount of blood easily drawn with that for the heartworm exam. Even if everything checks out A-OK, the veterinarian has base figures of your dog's chemistry for future comparison. Should your pet ever require surgery, these results will help the doctor tailor an anesthetic regimen to manage any risk.

Jay's eleven-year-old Boxer, Brutus, was slowing down and putting on some weight. Jay thought it was just age, but the vet suggested a routine blood chemistry profile (BCP). It showed high cholesterol, a sign of hypothyroidism. Further blood tests showed Brutus was very low in thyroid. Now he's on medication, has lost the excess weight and once again enjoys a game of ball.

Ask your dog's veterinarian about nutrition, dental care, pain management and other concerns when you are there for a visit. A doctor interested in preventive management will be delighted to know that you care enough to help your pet not only get well but stay well.

Dutch, a nine-year-old Keeshond, suffered from a laryngeal cough. The vet advised using a harness for walks instead of his usual collar and leash. This much improved Dutch's condition, which was irritated by the pressure from the collar.

INDUSTRY

There is a multitude of reasons to encourage activity in our golden oldies. Among the most important are maintaining mental alertness and strengthening the owner/pet bond that began during puppyhood. Making sure that our dogs stay active fulfills physical needs as well.

For every calorie expended in industrious working (or playing), one less is added as fat. The elderly's lowered metabolism requires less caloric density; even with a proper diet, it is still hard to keep off that escalating poundage without some physical activity.

Many of the other inevitable deteriorations of aging can be mitigated to a lesser degree by mobility. Sluggish circulation is revived. The increase in blood flow aids an aging heart, tired liver and flagging kidney function. Slow digestion is stimulated and a tendency to constipation can be mitigated. Use of the muscles helps slow the atrophy process as well as maintain tone for respiration and digestion.

Just because the old fellow is willing to sleep all day does not mean he should. It's up to us to nudge him into moving. Once in gear, he'll be delighted you remembered to include him.

The only cautions are to consider temperature and humidity and not let him overdo.

When involved in his favorite game of fetch the stick, he won't realize he's ten years old instead of two. You'll be surprised at how many new tricks your old dog can teach you.

From the age of six weeks, Cherokee slept beside Karen. When Cherokee was just one year old, she was diagnosed with severe hip dysplasia. Her owner thought she would not be able to show the fiery red Dobe in Obedience as Karen had hoped. Yet Cherokee showed everyone that the affliction was not going to slow her down.

Karen's kids had a trampoline in their backyard, and, of her own accord, Cherokee jumped on and off the tramp (about forty inches off the ground) at least a hundred times a day. Her highly developed

U-CD Mikara's Cherokee Maiden UD, WAC, CGC, age 9, doesn't let hip dysplasia slow her down.
Owner: Karen Ratliff.

muscle tone compensated for the bone disease, and the Dobe com-
pleted her UD at age four with regular scores of 196.

"Cherokee hated retirement and wanted to go to shows. Scent
Hurdle Racing filled the gap very well." At the age of six, she com-
peted in her first race. She continued as part of a winning team, always
an asset to the "Flashdogs."

Now she does demos and UKC shows, where the jumps are
lower. "Her most recent accomplishment was passing the AKC Canine
Good Citizenship test," says Karen. "She still sleeps beside me; how-
ever, we now have a waterbed, which she finds much more comfort-
able."

TLC

We all have limitations on our time, energy and pocketbooks.
Our resources are finite, no matter how much we love our dogs. The
amount of these resources we can devote to our senior may determine
the quality of his life once he suffers age-related illnesses. We must
each weigh and balance our pet's needs on one side of the scale with
our abilities on the other.

Every kid looks forward to the time he can have his own set of
wheels, but Sharon and Frank never imagined they'd have to supply
some for their little dog. Moe ruptured a spinal disk and became
paralyzed when he was five. His veterinarian didn't hold out much
hope that he would walk again even after surgery. But his owners
decided Moe was worth the extra trouble and opted for surgery. Al-
though the pain was relieved, Moe was a permanent paraplegic. They
ordered a cart made especially for paralyzed canines that was adver-
tised in a dog magazine.

Made of lightweight metal, the cart's lower bar holds the dog's
rear legs off the ground. The upper safety roll-bar can also serve as a
handle for the owners to "steer" the dog on a walk.

Sharon and Frank had to face the fact that they could never leave
Moe alone in his wheels because the cart could tip over or become
caught on something. Since the little dog was paralyzed, he lost the
ability to empty his bladder and bowels, so they had to take over where
nature had left off. She also takes precautions to make sure his system
flushes properly by administering vitamin C and diluted skimmed
chicken broth.

Patches, partially paralyzed with spinal myelopathy at age 13, is assisted in his physical therapy by young Ian. Owners: Ron and Connie Douglas.

Dandy, age 15, shows off his new "Dandy Pants" which were developed and patented by his owner for male dogs suffering from incontinence. Owner: Corinne Kuhn.

Sharon is content with their decision. "At ten, Moe runs, digs holes and has a grand time. Never for a minute would I hesitate using the wheels if I had to do it over again."

YOU

It is our responsibility to determine the quality of our dog's life. New technology has made it possible to treat many cancers with radiation and chemotherapy. Surgery may help in some cases. Others are aided by sheer determination—both owner's and dog's.

Patches was diagnosed with spinal myelopathy, which eventually results in paralysis. Connie decided that as long as Patches enjoyed life, he deserved a chance. Swimming was part of the Pointer's therapy, and each day he spent time in a heated pool.

For a time, Patches still retrieved his ball and Frisbee and stalked trespassing opossum. As his condition deteriorated, he was treated with acupuncture and walked with the support of a sling under his midsection. One day, while she thought Patches was lying in the backyard enjoying the sun, Connie looked out and discovered he was missing. Knowing that he couldn't have gone far, she finally spotted him toward the end of the yard by a fruit tree. "He was standing and pointing—he had cornered an opossum and her family. His determination and will to survive was so strong, he actually stood."

Complications of colitis caused chronic diarrhea and eventually dehydration. When he refused to eat, Connie knew it was time to let go. She called the vet and made arrangements for him to come to the house. As she prepared to take Patches outdoors for his final outing, he had a burst of spirit and dashed out the door ahead of his owner. He collapsed and Connie placed him gently on his blanket underneath the fruit tree. There they waited together while Connie talked to him about his life.

They had enjoyed more than a year after his fatal diagnosis thanks to their determination.

You *can* make a difference.

7

Slowing Down
the Clock:
Treating the Problems
and Diseases of Aging

Now that no shrill hunting horn
Can awake me in the morn,
Deaf I lie the whole day through,
Dreaming firelight dreams of you;
Waiting, patient, through it all,
Till the Greater Huntsman call.
ELIZABETH BARRETT BROWNING

TRYING TO DIAGNOSE SYMPTOMS in your pet is like the lawyer who defends himself—you don't want your dog to have a fool for a doctor! No matter how much we love our dogs, love alone is not enough to rescue them when they are ill.

Today's veterinarian has the benefit of eight years of comprehensive education, plus personal experience with hundreds of cases a

Sheba, a 17-year-old Weimaraner, is an important member of Lucille and Louis Delles's family.

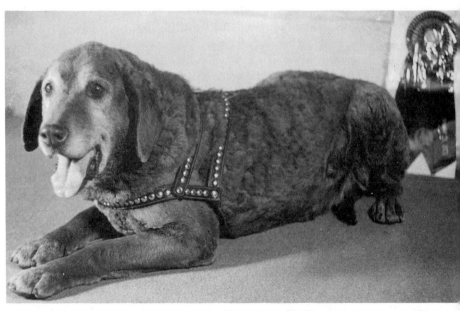

Chesapeake Bay Retriever, CH Eastern Waters' Dark Knight CD, TD, at age 12, in harness. Owner: Janet P. Horn.

week—and it doesn't stop there. Each private practitioner can call upon the resources of a wide array of specialists and research facilities at both private and major teaching hospitals.

AWARE AND INFORMED

This book is not intended as a how-to manual or to supplant good veterinary care. Being informed about disease and treatment, however, allows us to help our dogs in several ways. First, our canine friends cannot tell us with words when they don't feel well, nor can they ask for help by themselves. If we are aware of symptoms and what they might mean, we are more likely to seek medical attention at the proper time. Also, knowing the whys and wherefores of these conditions allows loving owners to become properly involved in home care after a diagnosis has been established. This adds up to a healthier patient.

Armed with this knowledge, we can pursue veterinary advice when it is needed, knowing that a health problem may not shorten life span. Many diseases or traumas, such as hip dysplasia, slipped discs or epilepsy, can occur at any age. Yet, through successful surgery or medication, the dog can live to a ripe old age.

Shelley's sixteen-year-old Lhasa Apso, Hoover, had one eye removed due to "dry eye" and has cataracts in the remaining one. She's deaf, has arthritis and a pronounced heart murmur, but, Shelley says, "she really tries." And Shelley has enjoyed Hoover's companionship for many additional years.

Sometimes it seems as if our friend becomes old overnight. Suddenly he can't see or hear. Yet our pet has probably been beeping signals to us for a while: that slower, more dignified movement may not just be regal maturity, but diminishing eyesight. When your chow hound no longer does a mad dash at the first rattle of the food bowl, it may signify a hearing problem rather than newly acquired manners.

People tend to associate disease with something visible or evident. Owners of old dogs often think that if there were anything wrong, they would observe the effects of pain or see an obvious visible growth. How often owners lament, "He never cried, so I didn't know anything was wrong!" Because diseases of age tend to accompany the "wearing out" of various internal organs, vague symptoms frequently overlap during the early stages. If we are observant owners, we will see these subtle changes and report them to a veterinarian so she can begin to establish a diagnosis of the dog's problems.

Diagnosis is the key word in this whole process of internal disease. Symptoms may be more significant to a vet than to an owner. She ferrets out signs on the physical exam that you may be unaware of and then proceeds to interpret the signals that the internal organs are giving through various tests. Only after compiling the tests' results can she reach a specific diagnosis. After gathering this information, treatment of symptoms and therapy can be discussed. With today's technology, we don't have to guess.

Not everyone chooses to proceed with expensive diagnostic testing, but each client should be given the option. Veterinarians frequently consult with experts in complicated or specialized cases. A good, confident practitioner admits she can't know or do everything, and is willing to say, "I don't know, but I'll find out." She may even refer you to a specialist or a teaching hospital.

The discussion of each condition in this chapter includes general symptoms, usual steps to diagnosis, what type of therapy is available, whether referral is necessary and what the long-range consequences are for both you and your pet. Your aging dog may never exhibit any of these symptoms or suffer from these problems, but if he does, an alert owner may forestall consequences. Fortunately, thanks to modern veterinary medicine, dogs who do fall victim to disease can still live a full life.

Carol Ann's Miniature Dachshund, Herman, lived to fourteen-plus years despite diagnoses of chronic heart failure (CHF) at the age of seven and cataracts at nine years. Carol says Herman survived many heart problems, most of which were self-induced because he was a little red devil. After diagnosis, he was given heart medication for the rest of his life. He had to live with the cataracts since surgery was dangerous with his heart condition. "Yet," Carol says, "he adapted very well. We said 'the nose knows.' If there was anything edible for miles he could find it."

According to his owner, Herman and his friends (Hope, a cat, and Honey, another Dachsie) were rascals, and Herman kept up well. With his failing eyesight, however, he refused to negotiate the basement steps, until one time when Honey dashed down to finish the cat's food. Herman couldn't let Honey have all the goodies, so pretty soon he conquered the steps too, making a beeline for his share of the dish.

THE SENSES

Most people who survive to a ripe old age will experience some degree of sensory deterioration. Canine age-related changes in the sensory organs are also likely, but dogs don't have the advantage of wearing glasses or hearing aids.

Senile cataracts are probably the single most common age change in dogs. A cataract is a condition in which the lens of the eye, normally crystal clear, becomes opaque. This blocks the flow of light into the eye and leads to dimming vision and finally blindness. Old-age cataracts occur very slowly and may even take years to become mature, that is, complete enough to obstruct all vision. They are not painful at all. You may notice a slight haziness, not on the surface of the eyeball, but deep within the globe. Have the veterinarian examine the eyes at your next routine visit.

Dogs have two distinct advantages over us when it comes to loss of vision. First, the dog's eyes are not the major sense organs. Your dog relies much more on the senses of hearing and smell as receivers. Therefore, loss of vision to a dog would be more akin to us losing our sense of smell—an annoyance, but easily adjusted to. The second advantage is that the dog, living only in the present, accepts the here and now as normal. Our pets are incapable of lamenting a loss of sight; they merely make the necessary adjustments complacently, without sorrow or self-pity.

When cataracts have been diagnosed, the veterinarian may discuss pursuit of treatment. Once the cataracts are mature, their removal is nearly as routine as it is in human medicine. It just isn't as common because our old dogs don't read novels, drive cars or watch *Monday Night Football*. If you want to investigate surgery, your veterinarian will refer you to a board-certified ophthalmologist.

As a dog's vision declines, we must make environmental adjustments to ensure his happiness and safety. A fenced yard or walks on leash are a must. A change of the familiar is discouraged—don't give in to a yen to rearrange furniture frequently. Introduce Bonsai to recent additions, or he may crash headlong into the new table in a usual path. Stairs may have to be blocked during your absence and, when necessary, climbed on a leash. He may require a lift into the car or a favorite chair. If there are other pets in the household, separate feeding may be advisable. Even total blindness is handled well by our canine buddies,

Snowball, age 14, hamming it up for the camera. Owner: Claudia Anne Zadro.

Toby, at 13, goes everywhere with his owners, even the golf course.
Owners: Frank and Peggy Adams.

Brie is an 11-year-old front-porch hound owned and loved by S. Rothenberg.

however, and with a little extra care and effort, will not affect either the length or quality of life.

Hearing also often weakens with age. This loss is usually due to degenerative changes in the nerves and is, therefore, irreversible. A special test, available only at some major veterinary medical centers, is required to accurately assess the degree of hearing loss.

For most cases, gradual hearing loss in your old dog requires no special testing. Common sense will tell you what's happening and will likewise steer you toward the adjustments you have to make. Be certain that Velvet is aware of a visitor's presence, for example. Awakening suddenly from a sound sleep to the smell of a stranger may elicit fear or even a nip from an otherwise stable dog. If she is awakened by you first and then allowed to sniff the hand of the visitor, she won't feel threatened and will probably just go back to sleep.

If she can't hear you call her back from the road because a car's coming (in which case she probably can't even hear the car, either), then you must make certain she is never near the road. Forestall danger before it appears.

"Shasta was a spunky Terrier. Being face to face with yearling black bears (tamed on leash) didn't faze her. A blue-tick hound across the road ran under a parked car when the bears were brought out," proudly recounts her owner, Esther.

Shasta was the first Australian Terrier to earn a Working Certificate and a Certificate of Gameness through the American Working Terrier Association. And how that little dog did love to go after the woodchucks. Esther remembers their sixteen-plus years together with happiness.

"I had many enjoyable afternoons taking her out to hunt woodchuck. Although I did not dig down to her, I would walk over the ground and listen to her barking underground. Depending on where the holes were, I could walk over an area of about twenty-five to thirty feet. It was interesting to see her come out and look for another entrance so she could get behind the woodchuck. Shasta was a very steady worker and would stay with the chuck as long as I wanted. I could call her out when I wanted to move on. As much as Shasta was an excellent working Terrier, she was not a hard Terrier, so I never feared her fighting the woodchuck underground. She was happy to let me know she had it in front of her and I was just as happy to see her locate it and listen to her."

When Shasta was about fifteen, though, Esther says something

Shasta of Triple Tau, WC, CG, at twelve. As is typical of Australian Terriers, Shasta lived to be more than sixteen years old. Owner: Esther Krom.

changed. *"I called her out of a hole and she didn't come. After that I paid attention to her actions and discovered she could no longer hear. It did not stop her eagerness to hunt; she was game right to the end. I just kept her on a leash most of the time."*

Owners can ease both their own and their pet's frustration by magnifying sounds for a deafening animal. When calling an old dog, cup a paper like a megaphone and speak loudly. Clapping hands and stomping feet carry farther by causing vibrations the dog can feel. Deafness, like cataracts, has no adverse effect on life span. She may not be able to hear you say that you love her, but she can still see the love shining in your eyes and feel those wonderful pats.

Comfort was always Spencer's top priority. Lynette says that every day, her husband walked in a nearby field with the fourteen-year-old black Labrador Retriever and a twelve-year-old yellow Lab, Beau. Here, safe from traffic, they would romp and play ball. One hot August afternoon, however, Spencer disappeared. Since Spencer had a hearing loss, he didn't respond to calls.

Fear and frustration were dispelled eventually when the manager of the auto dealership at the end of the field beckoned. There was Spencer. He'd pushed open the door to the air-conditioned office and made himself at home, comfortable and cool, enjoying all the attention.

Disease of the inner ear and vestibular mechanism (which controls balance) occasionally occur. Sometimes, if the onset is sudden, it can be confused with a stroke. Most vestibular diseases can be overcome with time and nursing care.

MUSCLES, BONES AND NERVES

Some inevitable loss of muscle strength and tone accompanies aging. Very few specific disorders occur, but the condition of the muscles often mirrors the state of joints and nerves. The old saw "Use it or lose it" holds true. Keeping up exercise is important for general tone. It is also worthwhile to maintain observation of the degree, progression and distribution of muscular changes as well.

Gradual muscle atrophy in the back legs, for example, is common with arthritis of the hip or spine. To avoid the pain caused by complete movement of the joint, the dog compensates by not fully using the limbs. Some reciprocal increase in the muscular tissue of the neck and shoulders may occur, as more body weight is borne by the sound front quarters. (Some oldsters with hip dysplasia or advanced spondylosis deformans have huge, overdeveloped fronts and spindly little rear quarters.)

Twitching, weakness or sagging of muscles may be signs of certain hormonal conditions. And a sudden wasting of muscles all over the body may signal liver disease, serious kidney decompensation or even cancer. With any of these signs, consult your vet.

Arthritis is another common complaint of the canine geriatric set. Rough, bony alterations inside the normally smooth, well-oiled joint cause pain during movement. The most common site for arthritis is the hip, due not only to the heavy load on this joint, but also because of the incidence of canine hip dysplasia, which results in arthritic changes over time. But arthritis can occur in any joint, including the neck, spine and lower back, shoulder, elbow, knee and even toes. Your vet might identify mild arthritis with a case history and movement of the affected joint(s). With more severe symptoms or a sudden onset, he may want to X-ray the affected area to rule out more serious bone disorders.

Arthritis in its mildest form can usually be controlled with over-the-counter pain medicines like aspirin or ibuprofen. As the condition worsens, your vet may prescribe stronger painkillers and anti-inflammatories, or nontraditional methods of pain relief, such as acupuncture or chiropractic, may be suggested. Mild arthritis can be handled well by most dogs. But a progressive, crippling form such as seen in many spinal or hip cases, and especially in a large dog, may limit the enjoyment of life. Eventually, some need to be carried. A clean dog will be mortified if he soils himself because he cannot rise to go out, and outdoor dogs may draw flies, then maggots, if they become dirty. All of these factors should be considered when making a decision on prolonging his life. While there is no surgical treatment yet for spondylosis (spinal arthritis), new technology has perfected total hip replacement in the dog.

Hip surgery at age five gave Natchez, a Golden Retriever, a new chance at living a normal life. Despite the operation and a subsequent fracture to the leg, Natchez recovered totally and has taught owner Sharon's other two Goldens the ropes.

Sharon had read about the surgery in Dog Fancy *magazine and determined she would buy Natchez that chance. "When I went to the credit union to borrow the money, and they asked what the money was*

Natchez, at age 12, glows with health seven years after his total hip replacement. Owner: Sharon Hamrick.

Moe, age 10, maintains an active life with his wheels. Owner: Sharon Henley.

156

for, the guy thought I was nuts! I would do it all over again in a minute." Natchez is now eleven and still healthy. *Sharon advocates hip replacement surgery. But, because of her experience, she is also a proponent of buyers researching their dog purchases and buying from responsible breeders to prevent the necessity of surgery.*

Bone cancers occur with much greater frequency in older members of the giant breeds. Early radiological diagnosis is imperative since most of these metastasize (spread) early and aggressively. If you notice a sudden painful enlargement in a leg bone with no history of trauma, report it to your vet; he or she will probably want to schedule your dog for diagnostic work immediately. Radiographs will be taken of the lesion as well as the lungs, the usual site of metastasis.

Routine blood work establishes the general health of the patient and the degree of anesthesia risk. If the lesion appears to be in its early stages and still confined to the leg, amputation to the joint above the tumor is the treatment of choice. Chemotherapy is sometimes added to the protocol. Although some owners may opt for immediate euthanasia, the radical treatment can be quite successful in prolonging a comfortable and pain-free life for your dog. Once metastasis has occurred, however, death will be only a matter of weeks. Euthanasia at this point will prevent certain suffering.

Very few specific age-related diseases of the nerves and brain exist. Senility and/or mental changes are usually due to strokes, tumors or medical problems elsewhere in the body. A senile degeneration of the lower spinal cord occurs in large breeds, particularly Doberman Pinschers and German Shepherd Dogs, although it is certainly not exclusive to them. This disease happens in many of the same breeds that are prone to severe spinal arthritis, and a differential diagnosis through X rays is helpful. Spondylosis is obvious on the radiograph and causes considerable pain and discomfort when there is a flare-up. Nevertheless, it also responds fairly well to medications.

Spinal cord degeneration, conversely, is generally pain free and nothing of note shows on the film. The symptoms include a swaying or wobbling rear and difficulty in arising. Once up and on a firm surface with traction, the patient can negotiate fairly well. Sometimes their back legs seem to get all tangled up as if they don't know where their feet are. In fact, this is exactly what is happening, as the nerves that used to tell the brain what the legs were doing (and vice versa) are gradually shutting down. Medications bring little relief and, sooner or later, paraplegia ensues. Since this condition is not painful, your decision on what to do will have to be based on nursing care demands and projected quality of life for a once active and now possibly frustrated or frightened paralyzed dog.

Nursing a dog, particularly a large dog, takes a great deal of mental and physical strength.

Donna's thirteen-year-old German Shorthaired Pointer, Winston, was thought to have "coonhound paralysis," or polyrediculoneuritis. Donna elected to try and save the old boy. She dosed him with the prescribed medications, "lots of TLC" and carried him outside a couple of times a day. She also says she prayed a lot.

After two weeks, she was able to feel some resistance when she helped him to his feet. His strength came back slowly until "one morning he just got up off his blankets and walked into the kitchen to my utter astonishment and joy."

REPRODUCTIVE SYSTEM

If your dog was surgically altered at an early age, then most of the age-related problems of this system will not be a concern. Even if the dog was previously a breeding animal in his or her prime, once the career in the whelping box or stud force is history, neutering is still advisable and should be their reward.

Intact females have a considerably increased risk of uterine infection as they age. When the cervix is open, either during estrus or at whelping, germs can make their way up into the womb. These bacteria then multiply and cause local tissue reaction until the uterus is a huge bag of pus. Pyometra sometimes causes a smelly vaginal discharge. A bitch with a closed-cervix pyometra is a very sick animal at greatly increased risk of developing secondary kidney failure and other serious diseases due to the circulating poisons.

Snowy, a ten-year-old Samoyed, was always at the water bowl yet didn't want to eat much. She was listless, and her abdomen was swollen. Examination showed her temperature at 103.5°F. and a greatly elevated white blood cell count. An X ray showed her uterus to be distended, and surgery confirmed that. A four-pound uterus (normally only a few ounces) was removed.

The treatment is excision of the uterus, but the surgery can be risky in an older, toxic patient. Victims are usually hospitalized and placed on intensive fluid and antibiotic therapy to control toxemia, and surgery is done as soon as the patient is stabilized. Why put such a grand old girl through what is so easily avoidable?

Other "female problems" include false pregnancies following the heat cycles. The associated milk production makes the bitch prone to painful mastitis (breast infections), which can abscess and drain. This can be treated medically but is more simply prevented.

The most dangerous problem for intact females is breast tumors. These masses are infinitely more common in female dogs that have cycled and although some start out benign, most eventually turn malignant. Metastasis can usually be prevented through timely removal. But recurrences of more masses are common. Sadly, some are so highly malignant that metastasis occurs very early, usually to the lungs or liver. These are generally untreatable.

Spaying before puberty lowers the incidence of breast tumors at an advanced age to almost zero, while spaying before the age of two reduces the frequency. After three or four heat cycles, spaying has no effect on the later development of breast malignancies. Ovariohysterectomy at any age, however, eliminates the possibility of pyometra, ovarian or uterine cancers (rare in dogs) and false pregnancies with their associated problems. This is one group of old-age problems that can be prevented.

Intact male dogs usually develop some degree of prostatic enlargement with age. Benign enlargement can be treated with hormones or surgical castration. Intact males also have a higher incidence of prostate infection and/or cancer. Treatment runs the gamut from simple medicine for infection to complex surgical and medical protocols for tumors. Testicular tumors occur with a fair degree of regularity in dogs, with fourteen times higher incidence in an abdominally retained (undescended) testicle. Although many of these are malignant, they don't usually metastasize aggressively, thus making surgery curative. Even though most problems of an aging male reproductive tract are treatable, prevention is certainly simpler and less traumatic.

HORMONAL IMBALANCES

In the aging dog, hormone glands aren't what they used to be. Sometimes they go altogether haywire. The function of hormonal glands is extremely complex and symptoms may be vague and overlapping. Although many of these glandular imbalances can be success-

At age 11, Chadwell Cover Girl's routine includes a mile walk daily, Pet Therapy programs and Veteran classes. Owner: Marilee Wilson.

Chances R Cool Hand Luke CDX, MH, won his Master Hunter title at age 12 and still eagerly anticipates his daily field outings. Owner: John and Nancy Miner.

fully treated, therapy cannot be instituted without a specific diagnosis. And in the case of hormonal disease, diagnosis requires a lot of testing, followed by more testing.

Thyroid Problems

The simplest in hypothyroidism, created by an incapacitated thyroid gland. An older dog with a bilateral pattern hair loss, dark thickened skin or one that is overweight and sensitive to cold might be exhibiting symptoms of low thyroid function. Testing for thyroid disease is fairly straightforward, and replacement therapy—although it must be continued for the life of the patient—is inexpensive and nearly without side effects.

Addison's Disease

The adrenal gland produces many hormones involved in regulating water, mineral and salt balance as well as producing the body's own source of cortisone. When the gland becomes partially nonfunctional through inflammation, scarring, blood loss or tumor, Addison's disease results.

Prancie was nine years old when Eunice noticed that the Airedale was reluctant to take her usual long swim each morning. At first Eunice thought it was just normal aging, but then Prancie began collapsing during their walks.

The vet suggested a blood test, which showed that Prancie had Addison's disease. With pills, Prancie once again eagerly looked forward to her morning walks culminated by a swim and continued to enjoy them for an additional three years.

Symptoms may include muscle weakness or collapse; increased thirst and urination; listless, nervous or dull behavior; shivering or even convulsions. When general blood tests point your veterinarian in the direction of Addison's, then more specific blood tests pinpoint the diagnosis. Most Addison's patients can take simple oral hormone replacement tablets that keep them in the pink.

Cushing's Disease

More frequently in senior dogs, the cortex of the adrenal gland does the opposite and produces too much adrenal hormone, a condition known as Cushing's disease. This is usually the result of either a functional tumor in the adrenal gland itself or one in the pituitary gland, the master at the base of the brain that tells all the other glands what to do. These tumors are usually benign, but they continually tell the adrenal cortex to produce more cortisone, which leads to symptoms of cortisone excess.

Owners will notice weakness, bulging eyes, increased appetite along with greatly increased water consumption, a pot-bellied appearance, thinning hair and finally loss of the coat on the body. Many Cushing's dogs end up naked on the trunk and back while maintaining a normal coat on the legs, tail and head—classic for the disease, but very odd-looking indeed. Again, specific blood tests must be run not only to make the diagnosis but to find whether the disease is of adrenal or pituitary origin (each is treated differently). Usually, Cushing's can be treated, either surgically or medically. Although some patients have a dramatic return to normalcy, others are not so fortunate. But most improve at least enough to make an attempt at therapy worthwhile.

Diabetes

Diabetes mellitis (sugar diabetes) is another common hormonal disorder. Although the hereditary and juvenile forms usually show up earlier in life, senile age changes in the pancreas can create late-onset diabetes. As in humans, diabetes is caused by inadequate production of insulin, a hormone that regulates sugar metabolism. Without adequate insulin, blood sugar (glucose) rises, soon spilling over into the urine. Thirst and urination increase greatly, followed by weight loss despite a ravenous appetite. Diagnosis is made by urine and blood glucose tests. High results in both tests confirm sugar diabetes. Dogs usually require daily injections of insulin, while a high-fiber diet (and *no* semimoist foods) may help regulate the stability of the insulin levels. The injections are easy to give and often dogs can live many years with their daily "fix." Diabetic patients must be monitored regularly, because there is an increased risk for cataracts, pancreatitis, infections and other secondary disorders.

URINARY TRACT PROBLEMS

The urinary system in the dog seems to be the "weak link" in the chain of internal organ systems. The great majority of dogs will probably have some sort of renal dysfunction if they live to any age at all. While some of the conditions are a minor irritation and easily dealt with, others are much more serious. Kidney failure is probably the most common cause of death in older dogs. Close observation and early diagnosis may make a big difference.

Many older dogs, especially spayed females, will begin leaking urine. Their lack of muscle control, especially while sleeping, causes their weak, old muscles to just relax and allow dribbling. Several simple and safe prescription medications, as well as adjustments around the home, help control this incontinence.

Sometimes in the middle of the night, Judie could hear her fifteen-year-old Pomeranian urinating on the floor. It was caused by being on a diuretic, and she could handle Muffy's accidents. But she said that the hardest thing was that people often asked her, "Why don't you get rid of him?" Her answer was, "He's always slept by my bed, and that's where he'll continue to sleep. We can put diapers on him, and he can sleep in my kids' old plastic baby tub."

Her friend, Barb, agreed. "When my old Dobe was eleven, we tried diapers, but she wouldn't leave them on. Mostly we confined her to areas without carpeting while we were away, but once in a while there was an accident. The neighbor said, 'Why do you put up with it?' and I answered, 'I can always get new carpeting, but I only have a short while left with Liberty, and she's worth more than any carpet.' "

She continued, "For years I watched the seventeen-year-old Cocker next door trudge out to pick up the paper and bring it back to her owner. Then I missed her for a few days. When I asked my neighbor if Blondie was sick, she responded that she'd had a couple of accidents, so they 'got rid' of her. I was furious! Come rain or shine, snow or sleet, for seventeen years, that dog had brought in their darned paper, and that was her thanks.

"You know, I haven't liked my neighbor since then," said Barb.

Rowena had an answer for the unfeeling suggestions that "he'd be happier" if she euthanized her twenty-year-old Lhasa, Sunny. She'd say, "Did you ask him?"

Infections of the bladder, prostate and kidneys are also more common with age and tend to create a burning sensation that urges sudden and frequent urination, often in small quantities. Stones in the bladder or chronic enlargement of the prostate also can provoke these symptoms. A differential diagnosis can be made with a good physical, urinalysis, blood workup and radiographs. While potentially serious, these can all be treated with medicines (infections, enlarged prostate), diet (stones) and/or surgery (prostate, stones).

It is vital to distinguish between incontinence (unconscious urination, especially during sleep), frequent urination (of small quantities as seen in bladder infections, and so on) and a true increase in the volume of dilute urine (called polydypsia/polyuria, often a sign of serious disease). This is something you can help establish for your veterinarian by careful observation.

A true increase in the total urine volume, subsequent to a hike in water intake, is one of the earliest signs of chronic kidney failure. As the kidneys become less efficient at removing the urea waste, the body automatically compensates by escalating thirst to increase the volume of urine and hence the volume of wastes flushed out. This compensatory mechanism can maintain a fairly healthy state for months or even years.

Kidney Disease

Other early signs of chronic kidney disease include gradual weight loss despite a good appetite, and an unhealthy appearance to the coat. Early diagnosis is fairly simple with a routine chemistry panel and a urinalysis. Your vet is looking specifically for changes in blood urea nitrogen (BUN), creatinine, sodium/chloride balance and urine specific gravity. Normal values in other areas help rule out other conditions. Once the diagnosis is made, a switch to a high-quality, extremely low protein diet (like Hills K/D, canned or dry, or an equivalent commercial or homemade diet) can make a dramatic difference.

Environmental changes can then help the dog avoid stress.

A veterinarian recounts, "A twelve-year-old dog was carried into our clinic. Thor had thrived as an outdoor dog all his life. Now he was so thin, he looked like a victim from a concentration camp. Initially, we thought he must have cancer or another terminal illness. The owners had noticed he was drinking lots more and that now he couldn't even get up.

We diagnosed kidney disease and got him back in shape with IV

San Sei Little Miss Chips CD, a Lhasa Apso, began her Obedience training at nine years. Owner Sue Rich believes old dogs can and do learn new tricks.

Caora Con's Bhan-Tara CDX celebrated her fifteenth birthday in 1989. Owner: Janet Larson.

fluids. Then we put Thor on K/D and recommended that he be brought indoors. A dramatic improvement was noted, with an immediate drop in water intake and an improved attitude. Although the weight loss took several months to reverse, two years later, the Lab cross looks great at fourteen and is enjoying his indoor life and special diet.

It is necessary to create a stress-free environment, have fresh, cool water available at all times and allow frequent trips outside. When owners are not home during the day, doggie doors allow access to the outdoors, or an area may be spread with newspaper so that his accidents don't humiliate him. One owner puts her Peke in a mesh baby playpen while she's away. This is not like puppyhood. He really does know better, but can't help it, and he doesn't like the mess any better than you do.

If the kidney destruction is halted or slowed, then the dog may function fine for a long period of time. Status can be assessed by periodic urine specific gravity, an inexpensive and simple test that correlates remarkably well with actual function. Luckily, chronic kidney failure is not painful. Most renal patients can live full, moderately active lives without discomfort or distress.

Sooner or later, however, more kidney tubules become dysfunctional and there is even less renal efficiency. Unfortunately, no crystal ball will predict how soon this will happen. While some renal patients maintain for years, others sink rapidly into total kidney failure. But since we can't know in advance, and the disease is relatively simple, inexpensive and painless to treat, it is always worth trying.

As the disease progresses to the point that diet alteration and fluid compensation can no longer make up the difference, nausea, vomiting and mental dullness appear. Owners may be able to detect a sickening-sweet smell to the breath. This is uremia, where the body is poisoning itself with its own waste products. At this point in the disease, humans would be undergoing dialysis treatments and probably be on a waiting list for a transplant.

Neither of these options is feasible for our dogs. Discomfort is minimal, and as long as the dog can eat, no immediate decision need be made. Often kidney patients die at home, simply going to sleep and breathing their last. A decision about euthanasia becomes necessary when the patient begins having mouth ulcers, internal bleeding and severe wasting, quickly leading to anemia, dehydration and starvation. In other cases, the kidneys shut down altogether, stopping all urine production and precipitating death within hours to days. At this point, most renal patients are withdrawn and mentally unaware. Needless to say, this is not a quality life.

STROKE

When an area of the brain is suddenly deprived of oxygen, through a clot or a ruptured blood vessel, it is damaged. These cerebrovascular accidents (CVAs) are also known as strokes. Because dogs can't have the problem of atherosclerosis (high blood pressure), strokes are not as common as in humans, but they do occur in older dogs. The symptoms depend on the area and extent of the brain involved.

Symptoms are of sudden onset and may include any neurological sign such as paddling, circling, aimless crying, pressing the head against a wall or object, dragging of a foot or leg, head tilt or twitching, drooping of the face, or even partial or complete paralysis. A massive stroke can even cause sudden death. Diagnosis is most often based on history and symptoms. No specific therapy exists, although your vet may give something to reduce swelling and accumulated fluid in the brain. Minor deficits such as drooping lids or dragging a foot are certainly painless and easily adjusted to. These symptoms tend to improve or disappear with time.

Even with severe symptoms in which the dog may look like he is on his last legs, many stroke victims can show dramatic improvement in a few days or weeks. But, during these critical days, a paralyzed patient will require a lot of time and nursing care. The dog needs to be carried out or even held up to defecate or urinate. The dog will have to be bathed and turned frequently and may need to be spoon-fed. Environment must be restricted to avoid injury, and fears and anxieties must be soothed.

Toffee had lived a good life. She had attained her UD and had given her owner, Joan, much joy. When Toffee was eleven, Joan noticed that the English Setter's legs seemed stiff at times. Then, at nearly thirteen, Toffee had a stroke.

Joan says, "She lost control of her bowels, and we thought she was crouching and shaking because she knew she had done wrong." But Toffee couldn't walk or even stand. The veterinarian diagnosed a stroke, but thought her chances of recovery were good because she was still trying to get up.

"For three days my husband carried her outside," Joan says,

"and I put a large folded beach towel under her body as a sling and supported her so that she performed all bathroom duties outside. She also wouldn't eat for three days." Then she began nibbling a bit from their hands.

Joan continues, "The fourth day when we opened the crate where the dog had been kept for safety, she took two steps out and fell. The next time it was four steps, and from then on it was uphill.

"She recovered a good 90 percent. Those last months she still seemed to be happy—her tail was still wagging. She would trot around in the yard, but when she walked she would stumble and lose her balance and fall, and we had to help her on the stairs.

When Toffee began to refuse to eat, Joan knew she had to make the difficult decision. "Her heart was good to the end, and as the vet had predicted, it was her legs that did her in." But Joan and her husband had enjoyed their pet an additional year and a half after her stroke, and Toffee had lived a quality, happy life during that time.

There are so many things our dogs do not understand and we cannot explain to them that life may become bewildering and frightening. If the size of the dog or your time constraints cannot offer this care, then the kindest answer may be euthanasia.

If home care is an option, it is best to ask your vet in advance for a time frame in which to see improvement. After the predetermined span, if things are no better, then a frank discussion of your dog's life quality is in order.

Another consideration with strokes is that once one occurs, others are likely to follow. So even if the stroke was a minor one, weeks or months later it may be followed by another, possibly more devastating one.

CARDIOPULMONARY DISORDERS

Heart and lung diseases are not the most common conditions in older dogs, but they are among the most difficult for the dog to bear. Age-related heart and lung disease is probably less frequent now than in the past because we have learned how to control two of the major contributors. Heartworm infestation, a cause of chronic, obstructive lung disease, can be universally prevented. Heart valve disease is commonly a result of infections caused by stray germs from infected mouths. Modern canine dental care and prophylaxis (cleaning) can preclude that source.

John Schmidt, DDS, takes his three seniors out for their daily walk. (L-R) Double-J Lemon Drop Kid CDX, "Chester," age 10; Teviot's Sparkle Plenty, "Mitzi," age 12; and Teviot's Appoggiatura, "Nancy," age 11, who wears a harness.

Nevertheless, dozens of other degenerative diseases of the lungs and heart exist. Dogs can have chronic bronchitis, emphysema or fibrotic lung disease due to poor circulation. They can acquire hypertrophic or dilating cardiomyopathy or other cardiac conditions that can lead to congestive heart failure. Myocardial infarctions (heart attacks) are uncommon.

Whenever the heart or lungs are not working to full capacity, there is a diminished oxygen–carbon dioxide exchange. Even mild deficits in this function lead subtly to gradual damage of all the other organs of the body. Chronic oxygen insufficiency will slowly and, if not reversed, permanently ravage the kidneys, liver, muscles and even the brain. These changes are gradual and often at first without symptoms, but it is these chronic deteriorations that—in the end—will be the dog's undoing.

Other early signs, therefore, must be taken seriously. Major symptoms of heart/lung disease can include loud, more rapid or forced breathing, pounding or rapid heartbeat, lethargy and exercise intolerance, and often a harsh, unproductive cough. General weight loss or a pendulous, fluid-filled abdomen may be obvious. As the condition advances, open-mouthed breathing, bluish tongue and refusal to exercise may ensue.

Blood work, chest films and a thorough physical will probably narrow the diagnosis to the chest. Specific diagnosis of heart/lung diseases may be difficult, however, without complex, expensive equipment found only at major medical centers. Some of these conditions can be treated with specific drugs or modern technology like pacemakers. Often symptoms can be alleviated with other medications or with diet. Many, sadly, are without recourse. That's why people in this condition often opt for heart transplants to start all over with new parts and an overhaul.

In dealing with a pet with chronic heart or lung disease, it is important to know that in the advanced stages, it is very frightening for the dog. When someone, animal or human, can't breathe fully, it is common to panic. Many of these pet patients have severe anxiety. They must avoid all stress, including the effects of hot, humid weather, too much exercise or excitement, too much handling or restraint at the veterinary clinic or the grooming shop and, last but certainly not least, obesity. As the disease progresses, dogs may pace, especially at night. They may be ill at ease while lying down, because they feel as if they are drowning in their own fluids. The lips may be drawn back in a perpetual gasp for air and the dog is withdrawn and internalized. If the condition cannot be alleviated, then the owner absolutely must make a decision about a pet that suffers extreme fear and discomfort.

DIGESTIVE SYSTEM DYSFUNCTION

The aging digestive system can develop several minor problems. Often digestion becomes more delicate and an overly rich meal may trigger vomiting or a bout of colitis. A high-fat diet can also provoke attacks of acute pancreatitis. If refractory, these painful abdominal conditions may have to be treated in a clinic with intravenous feeding for a day or two to let the GI tract rest. Recurrences can usually be controlled with consistent feeding of a high-fiber, low-fat diet.

The risk of gastric dilation/torsion also increases in those breeds with a predisposition, such as the large and deep-chested breeds. The cause of this serious and quickly fatal condition is unknown. The stomach begins to swell and flips over on its long axis, shutting off the opening and exit. Gases readily accumulate, causing gross abdominal enlargement and great discomfort. The victim retches continually without bringing anything up. The most serious aspect of the condition is the twisting off of the blood vessels, quickly leading to shock and death.

This is a true veterinary emergency. Immediate intensive care and surgery at an emergency clinic is essential if the dog is to be saved. Surgery to relieve the twist (and to tack down the stomach to prevent recurrence) is curative if the dog survives the immediate post-surgical period (the first week). Preventive measures for the deep-chested, larger susceptible breeds include two or three small meals per day, with rest and limited water following meals.

Big Red had been a first-class bird dog. When he was around fifteen, he decided to live out his retirement on an island with Mari. She'd had him a couple of years when he suddenly bloated. On the hour-long trip to the emergency clinic, his bloat increased so much that he appeared very pregnant when he walked into the clinic, tail still wagging. The veterinarian said the only thing that saved Big Red was his spirit.

Three days later, he had a relapse. Again, they made the heart-pounding trip to the hospital. The vet held out little hope, but that afternoon Big Red walked around the waiting room greeting everyone who entered. Mari says, "Not only had Big Red made it a second time, but in only a few hours had promoted himself to office mascot."

Mari credits Red's survival to the spirit of Irish Setters and to the fact that he was such a special individual that everyone knew it, including the veterinarian who took extra measures to save the life of a fifteen-year-plus dog.

Big Red survived to "hunt" sea gulls along the ocean, running as he loved to do, for miles. Mari remembers, "All along the beach people had come out of their houses. They were watching this special Irish Setter and smiling. They, too, knew he had good reason to celebrate life."

He also had one more thing: an owner who cared and watched over him.

LIVER DISORDERS

Several liver disorders can plague aging dogs. Because of the multiple and diverse functions that the liver performs, the symptoms can be equally varied. The liver chemically converts fats, proteins, vitamins and carbohydrates; creates hormones, immune factors, blood cells and digestive enzymes. It detoxifies the blood and is a major storage organ for many substances. The liver is also the portal of venous blood returning through the abdomen to the heart. If the liver becomes inflamed and swollen (hepatitis), there may be vomiting, diarrhea, inappetence, abdominal pain and a host of vague, nonspecific symptoms. Occasionally, liver disease is characterized by signs of temporary convulsions and mental confusion (hepatic encephalopathy). In chronic hepatic disease, the liver is cirrhotic and shrunken. Symptoms may include anemia, wasting, jaundice, chronic diarrhea and a potbellied abdomen due to fluid accumulation. The liver is also a common site of both primary and metastasizing tumors. Liver disorders are usually diagnosed through blood tests and radiographs or ultrasonograms, although frequently, as in the case of masses, exploratory surgery is necessary.

Many mild hepatic disorders respond to diet, rest, medication and supportive care. Once the liver is completely fibrotic or full of tumors, however, there is no treatment and life span is limited. Early or simple liver disease is not painful so long as the side effects (vomiting, diarrhea, prolonged clotting time and so on) can be controlled. As hepatic disease progresses, however, there are few alternatives, since the total function of the liver cannot be replaced. In the end, a liver patient looks and feels awful, with wasting muscles, yellow eyes and constant soiling. Unfortunately, they rarely die quickly, often lingering on and on. This is another of the conditions for which we must make a kind decision on behalf of our dogs who trust us.

CANCER

The tendency for tumors in all living beings increases with age. Our old dogs, like their masters, can potentially develop cancers in every imaginable tissue and organ. Some are more common than others, and each has a general protocol for degree of malignancy, rate and route of metastasis (spread to distant organs), and speed of growth. But since tumors cannot be identified by appearance or location alone, caution must always be exercised. Often in veterinary medicine, if malignancy is suspected and the mass is operable, excision surgery rather than just a biopsy is done. Dogs don't care if they're a bit lopsided here or there. After removal, the veterinarian can send a sample to a veterinary disease laboratory so that a pathologist can classify the tumor. Some of the more dangerous cancers have already been discussed under the organ-systems of origin.

The most common tumors are skin masses, the great majority of which are benign. Warts and fatty growths are commonly seen on old dogs and, because of their innocuous nature and frequent multiple occurrences, they are usually left alone. They should always be mentioned to your veterinarian, however, when you bring your dog in for a visit. A few skin tumors, such as melanomas and mast cell tumors, can be dangerously malignant.

Fred noticed a nasty, open mass on the toe of his old farm dog, Molly. Although she was between fourteen and sixteen years of age, Fred elected treatment. The entire toe had to be removed in order to excise the mass. The histopath came back "malignant" but of the sort unlikely to spread. Molly still assists Fred with chores and sits proudly on her remaining fifteen toes in her usual place in the truck cab.

Growths in the mouth are also common in canine seniors, and a fair number are malignant. These should be removed as soon as feasible just to make certain. Tumors are also common around the anal opening, originating from the glands there. They, too, are often cancerous and should be removed promptly.

Tumors can originate in any internal organ. Some are operable

Dream On's Follow Me CD, "Gandalf," placed in the six top obedience Schipperkes in the country at age 10. Owner: Laura Nichols.

Willie, now 12, lost his left rear leg at age 4. He was awarded Obedience Grand Champion at the county fair the same year. Owner: Beth Friichtenicht.

and others not. Symptoms, of course, depend on the system involved. Growths in the urinary bladder, tubes or kidney may be evidenced by bloody urine or decreased ability to urinate. Straining to defecate or bloody stools could be symptoms of cancers of the intestinal tract. Tumors of the liver might mimic signs of other forms of hepatic disease. Splenic tumors—wonderfully operable—only occupy space, not a serious complaint in the abdomen where there is plenty of room for expansion. This is not true of the brain or spinal cord, which are surrounded by bone, and tumors there thus destroy surrounding nerve tissue by pressure as they grow. These tumors, whether malignant or not, cause severe neurological signs. Often when a cancer has spread throughout the body, the major symptom is cachexia, a generalized wasting away of the muscles. The dog appears not just thin but hollow-eyed, raw-boned and skeletal despite a decent appetite.

Radiographs

If a mass is felt or is visualized on radiograph, the veterinarian often elects to do exploratory surgery to see if the growth is operable. Once inside, she can see the extent of the tumor, whether it has spread and how much normal tissue will have to be removed to afford a cure. In these cases, many owners make an agreement with the surgeon in advance: If the condition has spread too far or is inoperable the dog should be overdosed with anesthesia on the spot to avoid further agony.

Not all cancers are evidenced by a visible mass, and malignancies of blood cell origin (like leukemia) fall into this category. Diagnosis of these types of cancers usually requires blood work followed by a biopsy of lymph node, spleen or bone marrow for confirmation. Blood cell origin cancers are the ones most often successfully treated with chemotherapy and/or radiation treatment, and these protocols can be particularly effective for our canine friends. Although the majority of these therapies are still done at teaching hospitals, more and more general practitioners are gaining experience with the use of chemotherapy. As expertise increases, the more likely the treatment will be successful, with a minimum of discomfort and side effects and at a reasonable cost. Your veterinarian will discuss the options with you.

Fortunately, paralleling the rapid technological advances made in the field of human medicine, cancer in animals doesn't always mean the grave prognosis it once did. In fact, many of the age-related disorders are not the death knell they were in the old days. So don't put off diagnosis because you fear the worst—or because you think the vet will suggest that you immediately put your pet to sleep. Nowadays there are a host of options for diagnosis and treatment to help your dog maintain a long, healthy, quality life.

8

Paying Tribute,
Day by Day

If we are, as people say,
But the creatures of the day,
Let me live, when we must part,
A little longer in your heart—
   You were all the God I
   knew,
I was faithful unto you.
          ELIZABETH BARRETT BROWNING

SAVOR EACH MOMENT. Treasure the days.

That's what we all need to do with our dogs. Whether humorous, poignant or just the contentment of being with someone you love, we need to paste these times in our mental scrapbooks. Someday these scrapbooks will be filled with golden memories.

Reminiscence is enough for some people, but others want a more tangible keepsake. We live in an age of visual miracles: instant pictures, one-hour film processing, taped movies, video cameras. Yet too often people take oodles of photos from puppyhood through prime time, either forgetting or ignoring the less glamorous but heartwarming sight of a grayed muzzle and eyes that may not be clear enough to see two feet away but can still see into your heart.

Am/Can CH Follyhoun First In Line has won Otterhound Specialty shows, is OFA certified, and his breed's leading sire of Champions. "Sasquatch" proudly wears his Science Diet Veterans Medal. Owner: Louise and Rex De Shon, Jr.

Dust off the camera again and take photos of the old-timer. Sure, remember special occasions, but don't pass over Sampson snoozing on his chair, begging for a treat and other precious daily rituals. Years later, going through the album will trigger wonderful memories.

A little boy grows up and wants to remember the warm comfort of a dog that licked away his tears and warded off the closest monsters. A young woman recalls a grand old farm dog who not only helped her pen the sheep but had to approve of each new boyfriend before she was allowed to leave on a date.

Every time Tommie combed Spicey's beautiful white Samoyed coat, she kept the hair from the comb. When Tommie had enough, she spun it into wool and made herself a shawl, with Spicey lying near the spinning wheel keeping her company. Now that Spicey's gone, she's still close to Tommie and keeps her warm with her memories and her fur. "When I wear the shawl made from your fur, I feel love and beauty."

Donna suggests that everyone should look at their gray-faced canine pals and "think about all the wonderful things you have shared, people you have met, places you have gone, all because of a dog. I now realize how much richer my life has become because of dogs. And it all started with a fifty-dollar investment in a friend who is worth five billion to me."

The elderly dog has dignity. This is a dog who doesn't need to bounce around at your feet clamoring for attention when you have an armload of groceries. The elderly dog knows you'll get around to him or her soon enough. The senior has the wisdom of a sage—or at least appears to because of moving more slowly and looking at us deeply, burning an image into our hearts. From our dog, we get a glimpse of our own old age, and it's not so bad.

As the years mount, many owners celebrate their dogs' birthdays as they would any member of the family, complete with silly hats, dog food pâté, streamers and a decorated cake.

Even more owners include the family pet in holiday traditions—presents under the tree, sharing the Thanksgiving bounty, dressing up to greet trick-or-treaters. These customs become more dear with each passing year. There's no need to eliminate them because the dog is on a special diet or is too stiff to don her frilly princess gown. A crown or halo can be substituted for the dress and a small piece of turkey sans skin or trimmings in the kibble won't hurt. Traditions may be as informal as those within the family circle, or your old friend can be all spiffed up to shine in the spotlight.

In the world of dog shows, veterans are revered. These oldies may no longer strut the boards with their former bounce and power of stride, but the grace and nobility are still apparent under a crown of white hair. There is no doubt the Veterans classes are favorites. Busy exhibitors stop chatting and grooming to pay tribute to the dogs who have given us the present and the future. The classes always draw a round of applause and unabashed tears from all who watch.

Kennel clubs honor oldsters in various ways. Many Specialty (one breed only) clubs offer competition for Veterans in both obedience and conformation. Often there is a noncompetitive parade of titleholders where, once again, these very special dogs can have their moment in the sun. Devotees of the breed are allowed a glimpse of living history. They can see where those elegant necks came from, or the regal expression they breed so carefully for. This is their dogs' pedigree on parade.

Ads such as the one in Channel City Kennel Club's 1989 catalog express the pride of owners. "Oldies but Goodies," the caption for the picture read, "with hit records of their own," honoring the accomplishments of an eight-year-old Airedale, a nine-year-old Greyhound and an eleven-year-old Staffordshire Bull Terrier.

There are more reasons to show off these old dogs than owners' love and pride. Many veterans yearn to enter the arena again, eating up the attention and applause. Cindy tells another reason: *her fourteen-year-old Wheaten Terrier "had suffered a few minor strokes, but all he needed was the show ring (I doubt the lead was a necessity) and he was off and showing. Mine were probably the only dry eyes in the building, where he was on home turf being cheered on by his local friends. He didn't win the Veterans class that day, as he was in the ring with a much younger and equally influential dog. I showed him knowing he probably wouldn't win, but I thought it would be silly to deprive people of the opportunity to see these two great ones together one last time. Truly, my love of the dog himself and the thrill of showing him that day far outweighed any imaginable prize or win."*

Every five years, the ultimate show presents "The Best of Westminster," a parade of prior Group I and Best in Show winners. It is heartening to see how robust, sound and happy these retirees look re-entering center stage. Some of these are true canine septuagenarians at fourteen years of age, all still basking in the applause.

CH Raclee Express West O'Andover CD, ROM, age 14, still loves the applause. Owner: Cindy Vogel.

"Old Dog Night" at the GSDC of the Quad Cities for German Shepherds and friends.

J. Rich Johnson

Janet Repp took this picture of her Nariel Gallant Lad when he was age 17½.

A celebration of foundation Beardies piped in at the Bearded Collie national specialty.   *Larry Hein*

Veteran of the Year competitions are held in conjunction with invitation-only tournaments. Special Obedience classes for veterans allow titleholders to show off their prowess again, doing Novice exercises. Of course, they're so ring wise, sometimes they sit in one spot and wait for the handler to return. They know the owner will come back, so why should they walk all that distance? In their favorite exercise—the long down—no one ever breaks. They make a long row of graying muzzles snoring away the required time.

Why should busy people who have other dogs to show—youngsters who are in their prime and at the top of their careers—bother showing a retiree? Because a true showdog (as all these winners were) dances about with delight whenever the owner rattles a collar and picks up the show lead. Because they look forlorn when left behind. And because the old gal or guy loves it and we love them.

One group, the German Shepherd Dog Club of the Quad Cities, holds an annual Old Dogs Night. The special invitees are all over seven. These include dogs of any breed or mix. If members wish, they train their oldsters a while. Each dog is introduced by the owner, a brief history is shared and a picture is taken. Then a celebratory wiener roast is enjoyed by all. A member says, "We have fifty-one weeks a year and a dozen years more to work with our youngsters, but the best night in the whole year is when the stars shine again on *our* old stars."

At their 1987 National Specialty, the Bearded Collie Club of America honored its foundation Beardies, aged eleven to fifteen—those that were shown in the Miscellaneous classes before the breed was accepted into the Herding group to compete for Championship points. A bagpiper clad in a kilt led the parade of grand old lads and lassies around the ring. Knowing the sensitive ears of many dogs, an owner laughed through her tears, "It's a good thing most of these old Beardies are too deaf to hear those wailing noises."

A short paragraph on the individuals' accomplishments was read, and a personalized cross-stitched medallion on a tartan plaid ribbon was hung around each neck. Spectators realized history was in the making. This was the first and the last time these dogs who served as ambassadors for the breed in the United States would be seen together. Those who could not attend were invited to send pictures and biographies, which were displayed during the banquet. All present thrilled to the moment.

Another club, the Washington State Obedience Training Club, Inc., runs a column entitled "Over Eight . . . and Doing Great" in its

At age 10, Sultan Son of Pharoah can still model for the photographer. *Jerry Vavra Photography*

newsletter, in which members describe their seniors, sharing anecdotes on the dogs' activities, health and endearing traits, along with care tips.

When we ourselves reach senior citizen status, an old dog is a comfort—and not so exhausting as a young sprout. As Leah says, "My blue Great Dane, Sulton, and I are growing old together. He saved my life on three different occasions. If everyone were as good and loving as Sulton, there would be no more trouble in the world."

Velma, likewise, says, "My dog, Kizzmutt, is nearly as old as I am. Using the dog years vs. human years scale, if he is heading toward fourteen, that makes him about seventy-six human years old in comparison to the eighty years I'm heading for in April. Give us each another calendar year and he'll be eighty when I am eighty-one. He's catching up fast."

Senior citizens appreciate the human-animal bond even more than others do. According to the Census Bureau, approximately 95 percent of the elderly are *not* in institutions. With children grown and gone, and many seniors without a spouse, older people find an animal a comfort, a companion and a reason to get up in the morning.

"If I didn't have Frieda, I'd probably just stay in bed when my joints ache," says Allen. "But I know she has to go out, and that gets me up and moving. Then she needs her breakfast, so I fix one for myself and we eat together. After that she 'needs' a walk, so I have my exercise. By then she 'wants' to play a bit, so we fight over an old sock or I throw a stick in the backyard. Limbers up my arms and makes her happy. I'm not sure whose 'needs' and 'wants' are being met here. But I do know I need and want Frieda."

The complaint of many older people is that they no longer feel needed after a lifetime of working, caring for a growing family and keeping up a home. The job is over, the family has grown and the home seems to stay cleaner. Some actually feel in the way of society as it speeds quickly along life's Autobahn. A pet keeps us moving too, a bit slower perhaps, but at least we're not stalled.

Whether we're old or young ourselves, a dog moves along life's highway faster than we do and, if we have a dog, we'll probably have an old dog in a dozen years.

Chores that were part of the dog's daily routine become more time consuming, and sometimes it's just easier to do it ourselves or to train another dog to take over. But if we accept the slower methods or substitute something else, the dog still feels useful.

Am/Can CH Ranzfel Newsflash Am/Can TD was nearly ten
in this photo when he won the ECSCA National Specialty.
Owner: Virginia Lyne. *Cott/Francis Photos*

Sire, son and granddaughter sweep the wins in a Veterans Obedience class: (L-R) Robbie
Brooks with Heightland's Song of Shauna CDX, age 8; Ray Larson with Royal Baron of
Willow Run UD, age 10; Shirley Morgan with Pinebeach's Karate V. Glisando CD, age 12.
The Rock Island Argus

Tommie Lohmiller spins memories of her CH Trailblazer's Yukon Sunset UD. *Curtis Photography*

"When our old Weimaraner was younger, we taught her to go to the box at the end of our quarter-mile lane and bring back the newspaper. When Vi'let turned eleven, we noticed it was taking her longer and she looked tired when she returned," says Donna. "Occasionally she'd even lie down for a short nap partway back.

"But she wants to do it! Once I had my son ride his bike down for the paper, and Vi'let moped for two hours. So now, on nice days, the two start off together. Vi'let goes as far as she wants and my son hands her the paper on the way back. And on rainy or cold days, I drive down with Vi'let, give her the paper, and she contentedly holds it all the way home. I know the day may come when she doesn't care anymore, but until then, she still has her job."

WATCHING FOR CHANGES

As our pets' senses fade, our own must become sharper so that we pick up clues of aging or decreased energy and can compensate for those problems. Listen for nails scraping as they walk and for increased snoring or breathing pattern difficulties. Watch for changes in the dog's eating habits and visual or hearing capabilities. Keep an eye on the waistline.

We can treat many health problems through modern veterinary care. Other aging conditions are unavoidable, however, and can be treated simply by home medications (with veterinary advice), changing the diet or offsetting the sensual loss. One thing we can all do is eliminate stress.

All conditions should be discussed with your dog's veterinarian. If the diagnosis is simply "old age," there is no cure. Nevertheless, many of the symptoms can be treated. For instance, if she gains weight, feed her one of the foods for less active dogs or increase her exercise. If she is stiff or has a hitch in her gitalong, a coated aspirin product (such as Ascriptin) can help. To communicate stomping your feet, clapping and cupping your hands like a megaphone make up for hearing loss. Warn a deaf dog of your presence so as not to startle her. Be gentle and patient in your handling if she becomes confused or obstinate. Always walk a blind dog on leash or keep in a confined area. If she's prone to accidents, increase backyard jaunts and, if possible, carry her through apartment halls or in elevators. Any adjustments we can make to keep our friends happy are well worth the trouble.

We go out of our way for our best friends and grant them special

Sunny, age 19, shares his birthday gift with his daughter. Litterbug, age 16, sports a new haircut. Owner: Rowena Kenney.

Leroi, age 16, the inspiration for founding two humane societies in Mexico. Owner: Cecilia Vega Leon.

U-CD Olson's Bjorna av Bonbegard CDX, TT, TDI, age 9, good will ambassador at the Greater Milwaukee Norwegian Elkhound Association booth at the Wisconsin State Fair. Owner/credit: Kari Olson.

Granny Zestee CD, age 12, and descendents celebrate the holidays. Owner: Zona Munro.

favors. It's natural to want to cater to these old folks. All of the things that we were firm about, we're a little more lenient about now. Even if we've kept the dogs off the furniture before, we turn our heads when the old girl climbs up to snore peacefully.

Michael says about his Cocker, Taco, "To say she was spoiled is like saying Donald Trump has a few bucks."

He also says that he has learned a lot about buying and raising dogs since he bought Taco as a pup. He's discovered which questions to ask to determine a good breeder, that he should expect certain questions in return, the importance of researching health backgrounds (Taco has had surgery for crippling hip dysplasia), about the "miracle" of crate training and the necessity of exercise.

Taco doesn't bounce around the car like a high-perk youngster, darting from one window to the next or leaping on Michael's lap. ("I couldn't give you a guess as to how many thousands of miles she has ridden with me," Michael says.) She's content to lie quietly by his side, and Michael enjoys having her close beside him. After all, age does have its privileges.

Fortunately, several devices made for dogs of any age, such as the carts for paralyzed dogs, make life a little easier and aid our seniors in continuing activities. A doggie seat belt gives the dog more freedom than a crate, but prevents her from jumping through a window—or crashing through one in event of an accident. Harnesses distribute the pressure more evenly than collars when walking the dog on leash. Dog doors are convenient for owners who are gone during the day and dogs whose bladders aren't what they used to be. In fact, there's even one product made for a cat that helps keep small dogs from breaking training—a litterbox!

DAY BY DAY

When you live with an old dog, each day is golden. The day eventually comes when we lose our dog and that day seems covered with black clouds. We can live with the loss easier if we are aware of two facts. Because it may be up to us to determine when to end our pet's suffering, we should prepare ourselves for the possibility. And we have the right to grieve the death of a very special friend.

Glenda knew the time was nearing. "Laddie's last days were difficult for both of us. I have arthritis and so did he. Climbing stairs and getting in and out of cars was hard for him, yet I was of little assistance with my weak wrists. But somehow we made it. Togetherness was more important than momentary pain.''

She continues, "The last day, Laddie did not want me to leave him. Laddie wagged his tail but could not move his back legs. I phoned a vet I had known many years before, and he agreed to see Laddie. We spent a glorious afternoon in a local park. Laddie lying on his blanket, me absorbing the serenity, facing the realities of life. Yet I was comforted by the park's peacefulness as I brushed my beloved Laddie. His sable coat gleamed in the rays of filtered sun through the rippling green awning provided by the surrounding trees.

"Laddie was put to sleep that evening in my arms, best for him and for me. Neither one of us could give him the mobility he loved and required. I miss him and always will.''

Because of Laddie's qualities, Glenda now shares her world with two more Shelties. That is paying tribute.

9

Dealing with
Bereavement

NO MATTER HOW we wish our dogs would live forever (or at least as long as we do), it won't happen. Their comparably short life span is hard to accept—but it is for a purpose. Because no matter how we lament their loss, they would mourn us more. We are their gods and, as such, can we do less than be worthy of their worship?

We hope that our buddy will live a long, healthy, happy life, and we do everything we can to ensure it. Then we pray that she will quietly slip away in her sleep, without pain and suffering. Too many things can prevent that from happening, however.

Loss at a young age, whatever the cause, is tragic. But as we ourselves age, nature has a way of making death less fearsome than when we were young. When our dogs have enjoyed a rich, full life, we can accept the finality of their death.

Unlike people, our pets have a legal release through euthanasia, a release from discomfort or remaining years of confusion, humiliation or frustration. We need to know when to make that decision. We fear, "What if she could have lived longer? Is it too soon?"

When a serious illness or chronic infirmity has been diagnosed, it is important to concentrate on what the veterinarian is telling you about treatment, home care, prognosis and so forth. Once your mind has become more settled, ask your dog's doctor about euthanasia.

Although this is difficult for most people to face as too depressing or shocking, in the end, it will be comforting. We humans unconsciously tend to put bad things out of our thoughts. Still, we harbor fears about this decision. Most caring veterinarians will bring up the subject tactfully: "It isn't time yet, but with Buffy's heart condition, you may soon be faced with a decision about prolonging her life." Or "Reuben is really showing more signs of pain now. It's time you and your family began talking about what's best for him."

Although introduction of the subject may initiate a flood of emotion, or even resentment, at first, questions will usually follow.

Foremost, we want to know when the time is right. If no one ever talks about the end, it is hard to know for sure. The first thing to think about is the amount of suffering the dog is enduring. And suffering is not only physical, for mental anguish at soiling himself constantly or severe anxiety from not getting enough oxygen can be just as agonizing as cancer. If the suffering can be relieved or eased to an acceptable level, then that is a viable option. If it cannot, then you know you are making a kind decision.

The second consideration is the quality of life your dog is now leading. Dogs live only in the present. They cannot sit back in their wheelchairs and watch TV or remember the good ol' days while hooked up to dialysis machines. They can't even look forward to next week when a new treatment might be tried. If their here and now—the present moment—is miserable, then that is all they know . . . misery. So the parameters of quality of life must be measured by you, who have known your dog so well all these years.

The same characteristics that demonstrate your dog's delight from puppyhood on—a wagging tail, happiness at your attention, eating well—can act as indications of when and whether to consider euthanasia. One dog owner discovered a copy of an old Christmas letter in which she had written, "Rover's hearing is almost gone and her sight is growing dim, but she still has a very active stub of a tail and welcomes us home each evening with undiluted joy." Rover's hearing and visual losses weren't debilitating, and her owners were willing to make up for her problems by walking her on leash and calling her loudly while clapping or stomping their feet. That was very little to give to a dog who had given them nineteen years of "undiluted joy."

Sometimes it's a great deal more, however. Owners need to determine honestly not only what their pet can endure, but what the family can bear. Giving up a vacation trip, coming home daily at noon to take your pet out and dosing with daily medication are small sacrifices most loving owners are willing to make. Depleting a child's education fund to provide extraordinary medical care or quitting your job to spoon-feed and to keep your dog clean is more than your dog would ask. Problems that are workable with a dog of thirty or fewer pounds may be insurmountable with a larger animal. Carrying a Beagle up and down stairs four or five times a day is possible. The same task is more difficult with a Boxer and impractical with a Great Dane.

When there is no chance of improvement and the dog must be coaxed to move and shows little interest in food or water, it is time to seriously consider euthanasia. If the dog is in constant pain, is bewildered or no longer wags her tail or seems to care, it is time to give release. If she could, she would do as much for you.

When the subject is discussed openly and honestly and there is no pressure to make an immediate decision, most owners know when the time is right.

"Puddin's ticker began giving her problems when she was six, and we got medicine for that. At twelve, she had surgery for cancer," Mable said. *"Then she went deaf. I swore I'd never put her to sleep. Anything she had to go through, we'd face it together.*

"We'd made it to seventeen, when Puddin' had a stroke. When I took her outside, she'd just walk around in circles. She couldn't remember why she was outside. And she cried constantly."

Mable bathed Puddin', brushed her and put on the dog's favorite pink bow and, together, they made the final journey to the vet clinic. Mable said, "All of a sudden I knew that this was the time. When it was right, there was no decision to make. And we faced it together."

It has often been said that dogs also seem to sense when the end is near, much like the elephants who travel to their graveyard.

A few months after losing their old German Shepherd, Shirley spring cleaned the doghouses and discovered a treasure trove of Tasha's favorite toys, and a few of their other dogs' favorites as well, stowed away "as though she planned to take them with her and pass the time until her favorite people came."

More than one person has noted a renewal of a long-disappeared purpose in the dog's step as he prepares for his final journey in the car.

The emotions of that moment are tremendous and the dog sometimes seems to seek a way to ease the owner's pain.

Barbara said that when her Briard, Meriah, developed inoperable bone cancer, the old dog made her owner smile even though she was falling apart inside. "It had always been her habit to announce her arrival at the vet's—loudly and insistently—so that she was always given a private examining room and not made to wait in the large waiting room. She went in that last time the same way—loud and insistent."

Another reason to begin discussing the subject is that you need to know in advance what to expect. You should know exactly how the procedure is done, how the dog will react and what arrangements need to be made afterward.

Lassie, a fourteen-year-old Sheltie, had chronic liver disease. Lil and Vern felt it was nearing time to "put her to sleep," but when they mentioned it, Jan, their eight-year-old daughter, became hysterical. She had been told horror stories by her classmates at school about dogs being put to sleep by burning them to death.

Their veterinarian detailed the entire procedure to the child, explaining how the dog stops hurting and dies peacefully. The girl knew Dr. Dan and knew that he liked Lassie too and wouldn't hurt the dog. When the time came, Lil and Vern took Lassie to the clinic. Jan stayed in the waiting room until the shot had taken effect. Then she was allowed to see Lassie lying still on the little red plaid blanket that had always been hers. Jan cried, but she knew her pet was at peace and knew that Lassie hadn't been hurt.

Dr. Holly Bordner, a practicing veterinarian in Illinois, says, "I always encourage owners to stay with their pet for this journey into death. This moment is sad enough. To have a neighbor bring the dog in or merely hand him over to an employee is even sadder. Of course, some owners are embarrassed because they're afraid they'll break down and cry, but we assure them that we understand and don't mind.

"In fact," the veterinarian admitted, "we know most of our patients so well that it affects us too, and it's not unusual for us all to grieve together. This is why we feel it is so important to discuss the subject in advance. These procedures are scheduled, if possible, so that there are no other clients waiting and no feeling of being rushed."

Dr. Bordner explains the euthanasia process to her clients by telling them that the solution is given intravenously and brings unconsciousness to the brain within a minute, followed quickly by stoppage of the heart and then breathing. Unfortunately, the dog must be restrained for insertion of the IV injection. She warns them that an old, infirm dog may have poor blood pressure, necessitating several attempts. Although the dog becomes unconscious quickly and *feels nothing,* the body may twitch, the dog may cry out reflexively, or the bladder or bowels may spontaneously empty.

"This is unnerving, to say the least," says Dr. Bordner, "to the lay person whom we have just assured we are doing something painless. And euthanizing a longtime patient is traumatic emotionally, to me and the entire staff, as well."

Dr. Bordner's clinic, as well as many others, has circumvented this problem by giving a small dose of anesthetic first to ensure that the dog is completely unconscious but still alive, while the owner stays with the pet. This anesthetizing dose can be injected under the skin while the owner gently holds the dog. Then the owner, or in some cases the entire family, is left alone in the examination room to caress and comfort the dog until it easily and peacefully goes to sleep. This allows the owners to approach the normal grieving process with the best and most positive attitude.

Once unconscious, the dog can be taken from the owner to another treatment room and overdosed with specific euthanasia solution, monitored for a few moments until death is confirmed and then prepared for return to the owners or for burial or cremation.

It is comforting for the owners to know that the dog's final conscious moments were with the ones he loved most, with no anxiety from being restrained and manipulated by strangers. Nor will they have any unpleasant memories of normal but disconcerting postmortem physical manifestations. Instead, they will have the comforting remembrances of the grimace of pain fading from the lips, the harsh gasping for air gently easing, the tortured look disappearing from the eyes . . . the letting go.

Dogs have no fear of death or dying, and euthanasia is a gentler, kinder end. It is important to stand by your friend at that time, not because of the trauma of death, but because of your comforting presence. Your dog knows that when you're there, there is nothing to fear.

One owner said that the death was so peaceful she was glad she stayed to comfort her dog, and most owners agree. Seeing her dog slip away easily made her own fear less. "Of course, I was sorry she was no longer with me, but I didn't wish her back like she was in her last few days. I wished she was young again. That was impossible, so I gave her the gift I had promised her—an end to suffering.''

Preparing for eventual loss is much easier than at a time of crisis. Owners must know in their hearts whether or not they can make this decision and determine just what would be the most they can handle. Now and then, veterinarians will make a house call to administer the euthanasia, and this is sometimes easier on the patient and the owner.

Decisions must be made about burial or cremation. Many communities have outlawed the dumping of animals' bodies at a landfill or the disposal of them through a rendering service—and most owners don't want to do that anyway.

Much as the pioneers found solace in the work of building a coffin for a loved one, owners may find it therapeutic to dig the grave and bury a beloved pet. People with acreage and a succession of dogs often have a special Elysian field for their pets. Ken and Judy described theirs in a memorial to their fifteen-year-old Shorthair: HESS LIES BE-NEATH THE BIRCHES, ALONGSIDE HIS GREAT-GRANDMOTHER DIENSIE, HIS GRANDMOTHER BONNY, GREAT-UNCLE LINK. . . .

Donalee started with two "seven-eighths" Border Collies, Tiki and Samantha, who led to her current kennel of thirty Borders. But those two were always special pals. When she lost Tiki when both dogs were fourteen, she wrote, "I buried Tiki in a snowstorm. A privilege of living in the country is that you can work and rage and even cry to your heart's content. Samantha follows me a little closer now."

Should local regulations prohibit burial of a pet on private property, you might want to consider cremation or interment in a pet cemetery.

Many people plant a flower, bush or tree on their pet's final resting place. Some order headstones (advertised in major pet magazines) for the grave. Cremation ashes can be scattered in a favorite spot.

Tennis balls were sixteen-year-old Jacques the Samoyed's favorite toy. But, Marian says, "when he tired of playing, he'd take the ball to the yard, carefully dig a hole and bury it, covering it well by using his nose, and happily return with his nose well encrusted with dirt."

She goes on, "I found so many moldy decaying tennis balls whenever I dug up the soil in my yard to plant something. I recently planted a white rose at the corner of our house in his memory, and there was one of his buried tennis-ball treasures."

Society has begun to recognize and respect the bond between owners and their pets, and it is no longer considered "silly" to mourn the death of an animal. Books have been written about the subject of coping with a pet's loss. Hotlines offer comfort and counselors help owners to deal with their grief.

THE NEXT MOVE

Opinions differ on when and whether to buy another dog. One dog lover says, "I can't imagine being without a dog. I always have two so I don't have to face that problem." Another writes, "Losing a pet is difficult. Yet I crave the total, selfless love every animal has to give. Each time I've lost one, I've bought another one as soon as possible." A few are determined not to expose themselves to that particular pain again, but most understand that shielding themselves from hurt would mean the end of all relationships: marriage, children, friends, as well as pets. These people treasure the time with their pets, endure the mourning period, then begin again.

Linda has two old dogs she cherishes. She says it well: "Please don't ask me again when I'm going to get another dog."

Linda writes, "Over the years of our constant companionship, we've developed a near perfect rapport, an ability to read each other, to gaze into each other's eyes and know what the other is thinking. Such wonderful relationships are built only with time and attention. My dogs have spent a lifetime studying me. One glance tells them what mood I'm in. They read my body language like an open book. . . .

"I, in turn, study them. I try to listen to their silent messages. No human reads me as well as my dogs do. They are mirrors in which I can study myself.

"Even though they are too old for Obedience competition, they are not too old for a lot of things that are more important. And when they cannot do such physical activities, the treasure of their companionship will still be there. A happy greeting. A warm body curled up next to me as I read a good book. They are not too old to love and be loved."

"Man's best friend" is not a trite phrase. Losing a pet is truly losing a dear friend. Leslie says, "She slept beside my bed for fifteen years. During the night I would often pet her in my sleep. I still reach for her at times and wake up missing her very much."

Jo was at a large business function when the news reached her that her favorite pet had died. "I felt guilty because I wasn't there with her. I was upset at being away from home when I needed my husband and he needed me. I was depressed. I was angry. I was torn apart. But I had to conceal my feelings, so I'd go take a shower when I couldn't stand it any longer and stand in the shower and sob until the aching, gnawing pain subsided. I was never so clean in my life."

The grief of losing a pet is sometimes magnified by guilt (for choosing euthanasia or letting a pet suffer too long), as is the same sadness, anger and loneliness felt at the death of a human loved one. There is also sometimes a certain stigma attached to grieving for something that was "only an animal." It is never "only" an anything when the loss breaks your heart.

An additional fear haunts owners who believe strongly in a hereafter. Will they ever see their beloved pet again, as they will their human loved ones? Debbie expresses the prayer of most pet lovers: "As sure as I am that there is a God and there is a heaven—I'm sure that there is a green pasture where Max runs free." Poems, memorials and wishes of many testify to the prevalence of this concern, from the wistful "I hope Buffy meets me at the gate" to the adamant "If Angus isn't there, I'm not going either."

Some people continue to feel the dog's presence, hearing a collar clink or a pawstep when there's no one there, and strange as that may seem, it brings comfort.

Meriah's household was always peaceful; the other Briards knew she was in charge and accepted that. As her owner relates, "If Meriah wanted her spot on the sofa and it was occupied, she simply ran to the front door barking and the spot would quickly vacate in anticipation of someone about to enter. The others never seemed to catch on to this ruse. She also would begin to toss a toy about in obvious joy and when she was joined by the others in what looked like a great new game, she would restake her claim to the end of the sofa that had the view of the front road."

Barbara continues, "My husband has decided that Meriah is still ruling the household in ghostly fashion. Often one of the dogs will be lying in Meriah's old favorite spot and for no apparent reason gets off to lie on the floor. Or with no provocation the dogs will begin to bark at the front door as they had whenever Meriah tricked them. No one is there, of course."

Barbara smiles at the thought of Meriah's ghost tricking the others. Meriah is probably smiling too.

Another dog can never take the place of a former pet. Each one must be loved and enjoyed for herself. Don't make comparisons, because each dog has its own characteristics, faults and attributes, just as each of us does. It's unfair to the new dog, and it's unfair to the old one. It is human nature to put a departed one on a pedestal, forgetting any bad habits or naughtiness. There's no way a baby dog or young, energetic adult can live up to the behavior pattern that the old dog had a lifetime to learn.

Memorials release tension, let friends know about your loss and, many times, help others. Trophy donations, names on plaques, ads in catalogs and breed publications, and entire shows are often dedicated to the memory of members' fallen veterans. Clubs and individual members frequently donate a cash memorial to a philanthropic organization such as a humane society, a breed rescue fund, Morris Animal Foundation for researching a particular disease or the National War Dog Memorial Project.

If you obtained your pet from a humane society or a rescue organization, an appropriate memorial might be a donation to that organization in the dog's name. An endowment to the Morris Animal Foundation or one of the veterinary schools to study a specific disorder would be a fitting tribute to a dog who succumbed to that ailment. Veterans who came back home because of brave canine soldiers, as well as other dog lovers, can nominate pets in the honorary canine army to fund the National War Dog Memorial.

Veterinarians too are now giving donations to Morris Animal Foundation in memory of a special client's special dog. One such dog owner writes, "I will never be able to really express the feeling I experienced upon receiving a card from the Morris Animal Foundation saying Dr. Smith had made a contribution to the foundation in memory of Buff. My grief was considerably lessened by such a compassionate act."

Veterinary students at the University of California–Davis staff a pet loss hotline. Not only does this aid grieving callers, but it is helpful to the students in their education. The service hours are from 6:30 P.M. to 9:30 P.M. (Pacific time) weekdays. The hotline number is 916-752-4200.

Poems and stories written to honor oldies that have passed on evoke a powerful response. People with minimal writing skills seem to become Brownings or Twains when it comes to penning a memorial to a beloved pet. Even if published only in a local club newsletter, the writing serves as therapy during a grieving time. Write a tribute to an old friend. Create a celebration of remembrance.

Susie, mixed breed, age 15. Owner: Bob Fairman. *Mille Douglas*

Appendix

Human vs. Dog Ages

Dog		Human	
6	months	10	years
8	months	13	years
10	months	14	years
12	months	15	years
18	months	20	years
2	years	24	years
4	years	32	years
6	years	40	years
8	years	48	years
10	years	56	years
11	years	60	years
12	years	64	years
13	years	68	years
14	years	72	years
15	years	76	years
16	years	80	years
18	years	88	years
20	years	96	years
21	years	100	years

When are dogs considered geriatric and likely to manifest problems associated with aging? A recent veterinary survey compiled these results.

Small Dogs (less than 20 pounds)	11.5	years $(+/- 1.9)$
Medium-sized Dogs (21-50 pounds)	10.2	years $(+/- 1.6)$
Large Dogs (51-90 pounds)	8.9	years $(+/- 1.4)$
Giant Dogs (more than 90 pounds)	7.5	years $(+/- 1.3)$

Helpful Addresses

American Society for the Prevention of Cruelty to Animals
441 E. 92nd St.
New York, NY 10028

Humane Society of the United States
2100 L Street, NW
Washington, DC 20037

Morris Animal Foundation
45 Inverness Drive East
Englewood, CO 80112-5480

National War Dog Memorial Project, Inc.
P.O. Box 9126
Fayetteville, NC 28311

Helpful Phone Numbers

American Veterinary Medical Association
(to obtain a list of specialists)
312-885-8070

Bereavement Program
Colorado State University Veterinary School
303-221-4535

Bereavement Program
University of Pennsylvania Veterinary School
215-898-4529

Delta Society
Renton, Washington
(to obtain list of counselors)
206-226-7357

Pet Loss Support Hot Line
University of California at Davis
Weekdays 5:30–9:30 PM, CST
916-752-4200

Dog Foods for Seniors

Abady Feeds
"Senior Diet"
914-473-1900

ANF
"ANF-M"
800-722-3261

Bench and Field
"20%"
800-525-4802

Bil-Jac
"Lite"
800-321-1002

Gaines
"Cycle 3" and "Cycle 4"
800-942-0332

Hills
prescription diets
800-548-8387

Iams
"Less Active"
800-525-4267

Natural Life
"Senior Dog Formula"
800-367-2391

Nature's Recipe
"Senior/Pension"
714-639-1134

Nutro
"Max Special"
800-833-5330

Purina Pro-Plan
"Lite"
800-PRO-LITE

Royal Canin
"Senior Croquettes"
800-592-6687

Science Diet
"Maintenance Light"
"Senior"
800-445-5777

Techni-Cal
"Lite" and "Senior"
800-265-3370

Books and tapes of further interest

Anderson, Moira K.
Coping With Sorrow on The Loss of Your Pet
Peregrine Press
12228 Venice Blvd., Suite 380
Los Angeles, CA 90066

Church, Julie Adams
Joy In A Woolly Coat
H. J. Kramer, Inc.
P.O. Box 1082
Tiburon, CA 94920

Kay, W. J., H. A. Nieburg, A. H. Kutscher, R. M. Grey and C. E. Fudin
Pet Loss and Human Bereavement
Iowa State University Press
Ames, IA 50010

McLennan, Bardi
"Recycled Pet" and "Your Dog's Final Years"
The Canine Consultant series of audiotapes
Bardwyn Productions, Inc.
25 Van Zant Street
East Norwalk, CT 06855
203-853-4011

Neiburg, Herbert A. and Arlene Fischer
Pet Loss: A Thoughtful Guide for Adults and Children
Harper and Row Publishers, Inc.
10 E. 53rd St.
New York, NY 10020

Quackenbush, Jamie, M.S.W. and Denise Graveline
When Your Pet Dies
Simon and Schuster
1230 Ave. of the Americas
New York, NY 10020

Products of Interest (These are examples; readers will find many others in the ad sections of major dog magazines.)

Cat Nap
heated, washable cushion bed
3020 Bridgeway, Suite 177
Sausalito, CA 94965
415-331-5293

Everlasting Stone Products, Co.
grave markers and monuments
P.O. Box 995
Barre, VT 05641
800-882-6686

Fiber Formula
low-fat, high-fiber dog biscuit treats
800-234-0322

Hale Security Pet Door
5622 N. 52nd Ave., #4
Glendale, AZ 85301
800-888-8914

KK Products
Dandy Pants, for incontinent dogs
1935 Squires Way Ct.
Chesterfield, MO 63017
314-532-4007

K-9 Carts
custom-made "wheels" for paralyzed dogs
532 Newtown Road
Berwyn, PA 19312
215-644-6624

Nylabone Products
Myti-Bone, softer chew product for older dogs
Box 427
Neptune, NJ 07753

Pup-E-Luv
white cedar dog bed
2395 Colorado Ave.
North Bend, OR 97459
800-338-7227